INSIDE DINOSAURS
AND OTHER
PREHISTORIC CREATURES

INSIDE DINOSAURS
AND OTHER
PREHISTORIC CREATURES

Illustrated by Ted Dewan
Written by Steve Parker

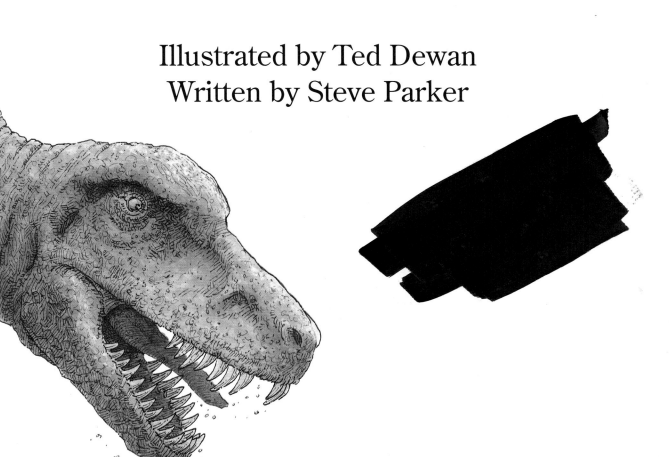

A DOUBLEDAY BOOK FOR YOUNG READERS

A Dorling Kindersley Book

Project Editor   Laura Buller
Art Editors   Sarah Ponder
              Diane Clouting
Production   Susannah Straughan
Consultant   William Lindsay
Managing Editor   Helen Parker
Managing Art Editor   Peter Bailey

A Doubleday Book for Young Readers

Published by Delacorte Press, Bantam Doubleday Dell Publishing Group, Inc.
1540 Broadway, New York, New York 10036

Doubleday and the portrayal of an anchor with a dolphin are trademarks of Bantam Doubleday Dell Publishing Group, Inc.

First published in Great Britain in 1993 by Dorling Kindersley Limited, 9 Henrietta Street, London WC2E 8PS

Library of Congress Cataloging in Publication Data

Parker, Steve.
    Inside dinosaurs and other prehistoric creatures / written by Steve Parker : illustrated by Ted Dewan
       p.   cm.
    "A Doubleday book for young readers."
    Includes index.
    Summary: Text and cutaway illustrations depict the outer and inner anatomy of dinosaurs and other prehistoric animals.
    ISBN 0-385-31143-5. — ISBN 0-385-31189-3 (pbk.)
    1. Dinosaurs—Anatomy—Juvenile literature. 2. Animals, fossil—Anatomy—Juvenile literature. [1. Dinosaurs—Anatomy.
2. Prehistoric animals—Anatomy.] I. Dewan, Ted, ill. II. Title.
III. Title: Inside dinosaurs.
QE862.D5P1465 1994
667.9'1—dc20
                           93-10045
                           CIP
                           AC

Reproduced in Essex by Dot Gradations
Printed in Italy by A. Mondadori Editore, Verona
April 1994
10 9 8 7 6 5 4 3 2 1

To Gramps—the greatest dinosaur in 64 million years—T.D.

*To the memory of my father, Ron,
who would have been proud—but puzzled!—S.P.*

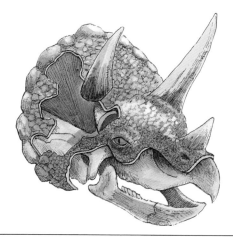

CONTENTS

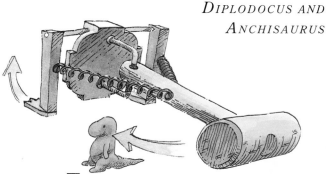

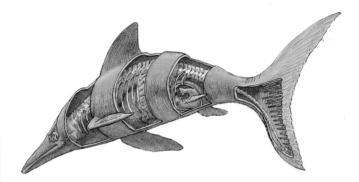

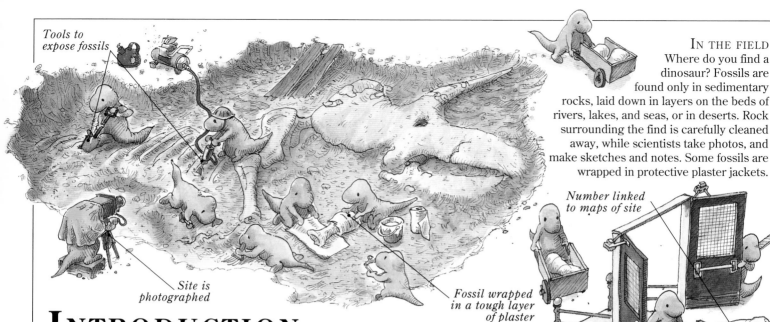

Tools to expose fossils

Site is photographed

Fossil wrapped in a tough layer of plaster

IN THE FIELD
Where do you find a dinosaur? Fossils are found only in sedimentary rocks, laid down in layers on the beds of rivers, lakes, and seas, or in deserts. Rock surrounding the find is carefully cleaned away, while scientists take photos, and make sketches and notes. Some fossils are wrapped in protective plaster jackets.

Number linked to maps of site

INTRODUCTION

INSIDE A DINOSAUR? You're kidding! No one ever saw a living, breathing dinosaur—not even a caveperson, since the last dinos died more than sixty million years before the first humans appeared. All that is left of these creatures are bones, teeth, horns, and claws, which turned to stone and formed fossils.

But fossils are valuable clues. For instance, we know from today's animals that flat-topped teeth are for chewing tough plant food. Long, pointy teeth are designed to kill. Straightaway, just one fossil tooth can identify its owner as a plant eater or hunter. Weird and wonderful fossils of dinosaur eggs, last dinners, and dino droppings give further glimpses of their living habits. The remains of other animals and plants found with the fossils, and the rocks surrounding them, tell us about the place a dinosaur called home. Of course, there is still plenty of guesswork. Soft parts, such as brains, hearts, and skin, rarely fossilized. But a little detective work can bring a dino back to life…well, almost.

Our previous book, *Inside the Whale and Other Animals*, took animals apart from the outside in. This book puts animals back together, from the inside out. The dinosaurs and other featured creatures that stalked, swam, flew, ran, and lumbered over the planet will give you a peek into the strange and ferocious world that was prehistoric Earth.

Ted Dewan

Steve Parker

BACK TO THE LAB
A huge dinosaur fossil is solid rock—so it's very heavy. It may be a long, hard road from a remote fossil site to the comfort of the workshop.

CHECK IN
The fossils are carefully unwrapped and checked. All finds are cataloged and numbered. Your fossil might make headlines, so you'd better not lose it!

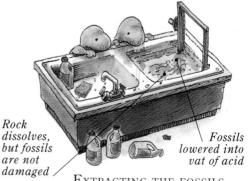

Rock dissolves, but fossils are not damaged

Fossils lowered into vat of acid

EXTRACTING THE FOSSILS
Experts use various methods to clear away the rock around the fossil, including acid baths.

Only newsworthy fossils get instant attention—others go to the vaults.

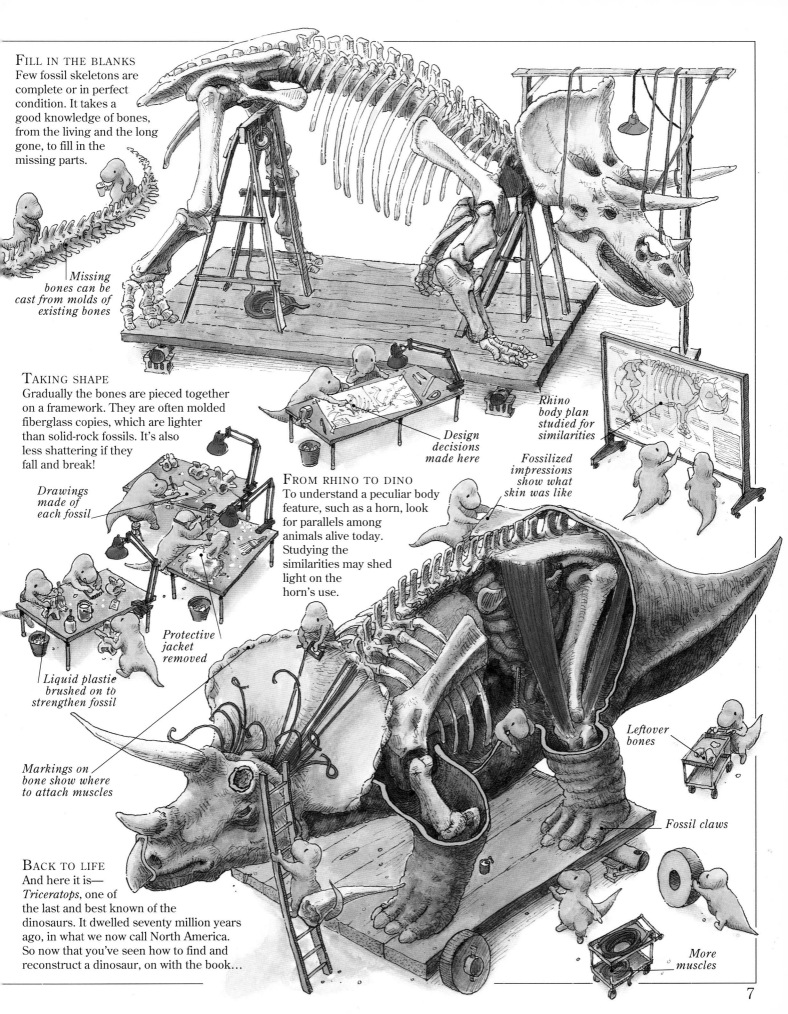

FILL IN THE BLANKS
Few fossil skeletons are
complete or in perfect
condition. It takes a
good knowledge of bones,
from the living and the long
gone, to fill in the
missing parts.

*Missing
bones can be
cast from molds of
existing bones*

TAKING SHAPE
Gradually the bones are pieced together
on a framework. They are often molded
fiberglass copies, which are lighter
than solid-rock fossils. It's also
less shattering if they
fall and break!

*Drawings
made of
each fossil*

*Liquid plastic
brushed on to
strengthen fossil*

*Protective
jacket
removed*

FROM RHINO TO DINO
To understand a peculiar body
feature, such as a horn, look
for parallels among
animals alive today.
Studying the
similarities may shed
light on the
horn's use.

*Design
decisions
made here*

*Rhino
body plan
studied for
similarities*

*Fossilized
impressions
show what
skin was like*

*Markings on
bone show where
to attach muscles*

*Leftover
bones*

Fossil claws

BACK TO LIFE
And here it is—
Triceratops, one of
the last and best known of the
dinosaurs. It dwelled seventy million years
ago, in what we now call North America.
So now that you've seen how to find and
reconstruct a dinosaur, on with the book…

*More
muscles*

READING THE BONES

MOST OF WHAT WE THINK WE KNOW about dinosaurs comes from the study of their preserved remains: chiefly bones, teeth, horns, and claws. These provide several clues. From just a few fossil bones, for example, you can make a good stab at the creature's overall size. The fossil's shape gives even more clues. If you have a working knowledge of similar animal skeletons, living and extinct, you can assign a bone to a body part by its shape alone. Surface details lead to other discoveries. Ridges, rough or smooth patches, holes, and grooves indicate the positions of muscle and tendon attachments, nerves, and blood vessels. Gradually, the pieces of the jigsaw fit together and produce something more: a picture of the dinosaur's behavior and way of life.

CRESTS AND RIDGES
Lumps, crests, and ridges on bones like the bump on this thighbone imply muscle attachments—especially if the surface is roughened and pitted in texture. This was where the muscle's tendon grew into and anchored on the bone, for strength and pulling power. The bumps and flanges provided extra surface area, and angled the bone's surface so that the muscle could pull it more efficiently.

IGUANODON
This 33-foot (10-meter)-long beast from 120 million years ago was one of the first dinosaurs to be officially named and described—on the evidence of teeth alone. English doctor and fossil hunter Gideon Mantell with his wife Mary Ann found the teeth in about 1821. Noting their similarity to those of an iguana lizard, he described the owner of the teeth in 1825 as *Iguanodon* ("iguana tooth").

MISSING PIECES
If you had a nearly-finished jigsaw, you could probably guess what the missing pieces looked like. A fossil skeleton is rarely complete. So in the same way, missing parts are reconstructed, or borrowed from other, similar dinosaurs. A missing tail vertebra (backbone), for example, could be mocked up following a standard tapering pattern.

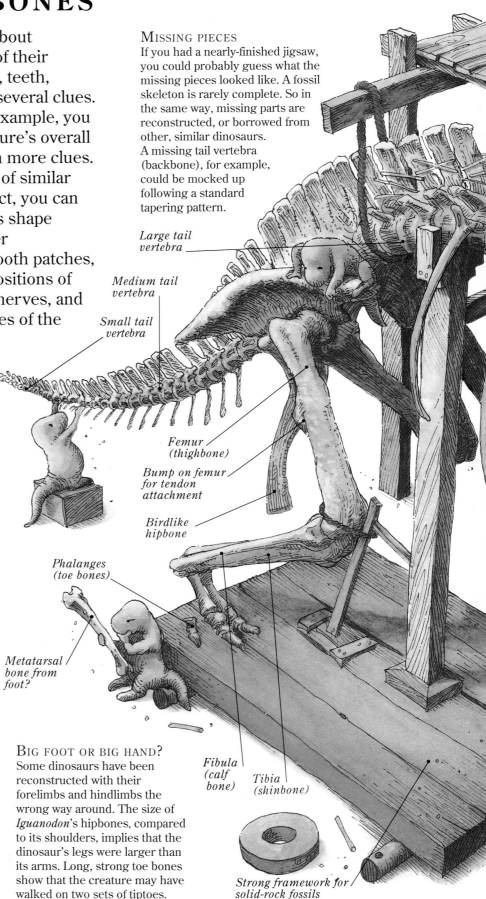

Large tail vertebra

Medium tail vertebra

Small tail vertebra

Femur (thighbone)

Bump on femur for tendon attachment

Birdlike hipbone

Phalanges (toe bones)

Metatarsal bone from foot?

Fibula (calf bone)

Tibia (shinbone)

Strong framework for solid-rock fossils

BIG FOOT OR BIG HAND?
Some dinosaurs have been reconstructed with their forelimbs and hindlimbs the wrong way around. The size of *Iguanodon*'s hipbones, compared to its shoulders, implies that the dinosaur's legs were larger than its arms. Long, strong toe bones show that the creature may have walked on two sets of tiptoes.

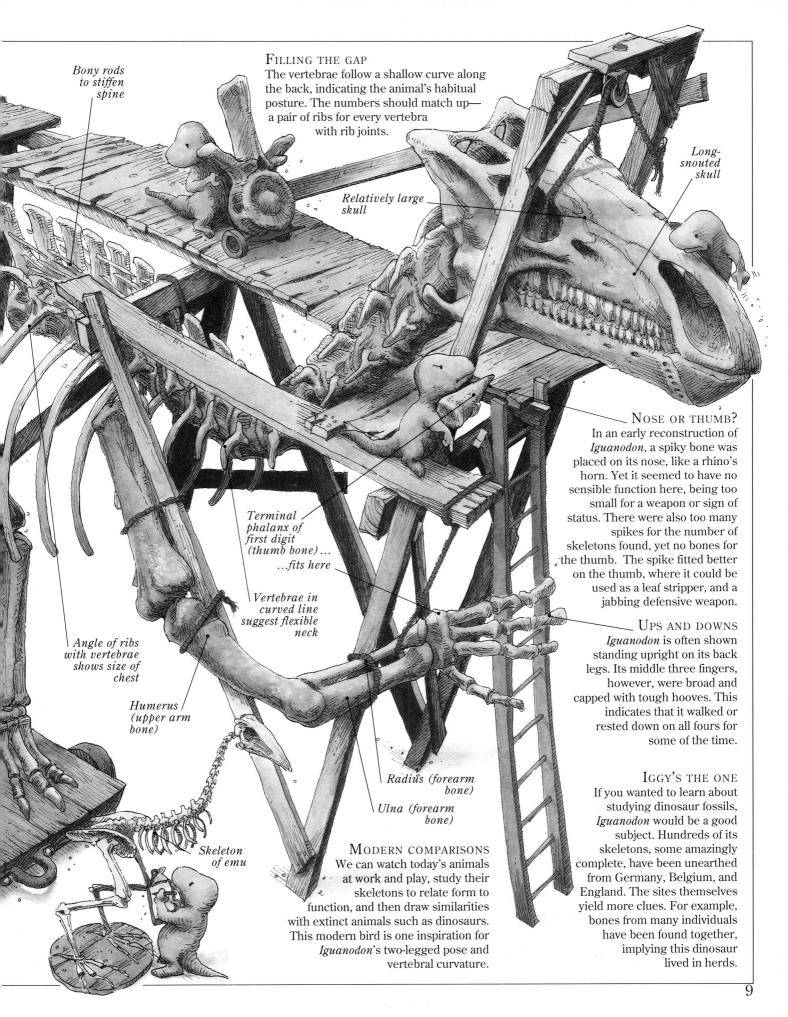

Bony rods to stiffen spine

FILLING THE GAP
The vertebrae follow a shallow curve along the back, indicating the animal's habitual posture. The numbers should match up— a pair of ribs for every vertebra with rib joints.

Relatively large skull

Long-snouted skull

Terminal phalanx of first digit (thumb bone) ...
...fits here

Vertebrae in curved line suggest flexible neck

Angle of ribs with vertebrae shows size of chest

Humerus (upper arm bone)

Skeleton of emu

Radius (forearm bone)

Ulna (forearm bone)

NOSE OR THUMB?
In an early reconstruction of *Iguanodon*, a spiky bone was placed on its nose, like a rhino's horn. Yet it seemed to have no sensible function here, being too small for a weapon or sign of status. There were also too many spikes for the number of skeletons found, yet no bones for the thumb. The spike fitted better on the thumb, where it could be used as a leaf stripper, and a jabbing defensive weapon.

UPS AND DOWNS
Iguanodon is often shown standing upright on its back legs. Its middle three fingers, however, were broad and capped with tough hooves. This indicates that it walked or rested down on all fours for some of the time.

IGGY'S THE ONE
If you wanted to learn about studying dinosaur fossils, *Iguanodon* would be a good subject. Hundreds of its skeletons, some amazingly complete, have been unearthed from Germany, Belgium, and England. The sites themselves yield more clues. For example, bones from many individuals have been found together, implying this dinosaur lived in herds.

MODERN COMPARISONS
We can watch today's animals at work and play, study their skeletons to relate form to function, and then draw similarities with extinct animals such as dinosaurs. This modern bird is one inspiration for *Iguanodon*'s two-legged pose and vertebral curvature.

9

TEETH AND JAWS

BEING TRAPPED IN THE TEETH of *Tyrannosaurus* was no joke. Rows of daggers longer than your hand, with edges serrated like steak knives, biting with crushing force, could chop through your arm in an instant. Dinosaur teeth, being very hard, make excellent fossils. Their sizes, shapes, and positions in the jaws provide vital clues to favorite foods. They show if a dinosaur was a meat-slicing carnivore or a plant-crushing herbivore.

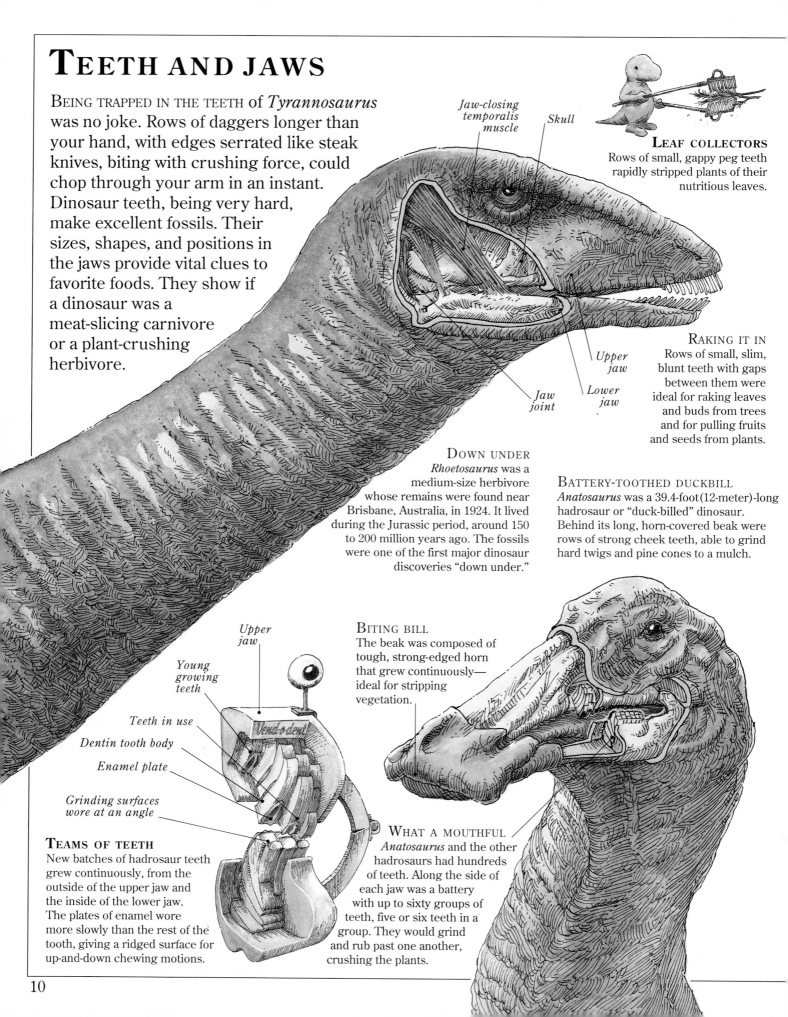

Jaw-closing temporalis muscle

Skull

Upper jaw

Lower jaw

Jaw joint

LEAF COLLECTORS
Rows of small, gappy peg teeth rapidly stripped plants of their nutritious leaves.

RAKING IT IN
Rows of small, slim, blunt teeth with gaps between them were ideal for raking leaves and buds from trees and for pulling fruits and seeds from plants.

DOWN UNDER
Rhoetosaurus was a medium-size herbivore whose remains were found near Brisbane, Australia, in 1924. It lived during the Jurassic period, around 150 to 200 million years ago. The fossils were one of the first major dinosaur discoveries "down under."

BATTERY-TOOTHED DUCKBILL
Anatosaurus was a 39.4-foot (12-meter)-long hadrosaur or "duck-billed" dinosaur. Behind its long, horn-covered beak were rows of strong cheek teeth, able to grind hard twigs and pine cones to a mulch.

Upper jaw

Young growing teeth

Teeth in use

Dentin tooth body

Enamel plate

Grinding surfaces wore at an angle

Vend-o-dent

BITING BILL
The beak was composed of tough, strong-edged horn that grew continuously—ideal for stripping vegetation.

TEAMS OF TEETH
New batches of hadrosaur teeth grew continuously, from the outside of the upper jaw and the inside of the lower jaw. The plates of enamel wore more slowly than the rest of the tooth, giving a ridged surface for up-and-down chewing motions.

WHAT A MOUTHFUL
Anatosaurus and the other hadrosaurs had hundreds of teeth. Along the side of each jaw was a battery with up to sixty groups of teeth, five or six teeth in a group. They would grind and rub past one another, crushing the plants.

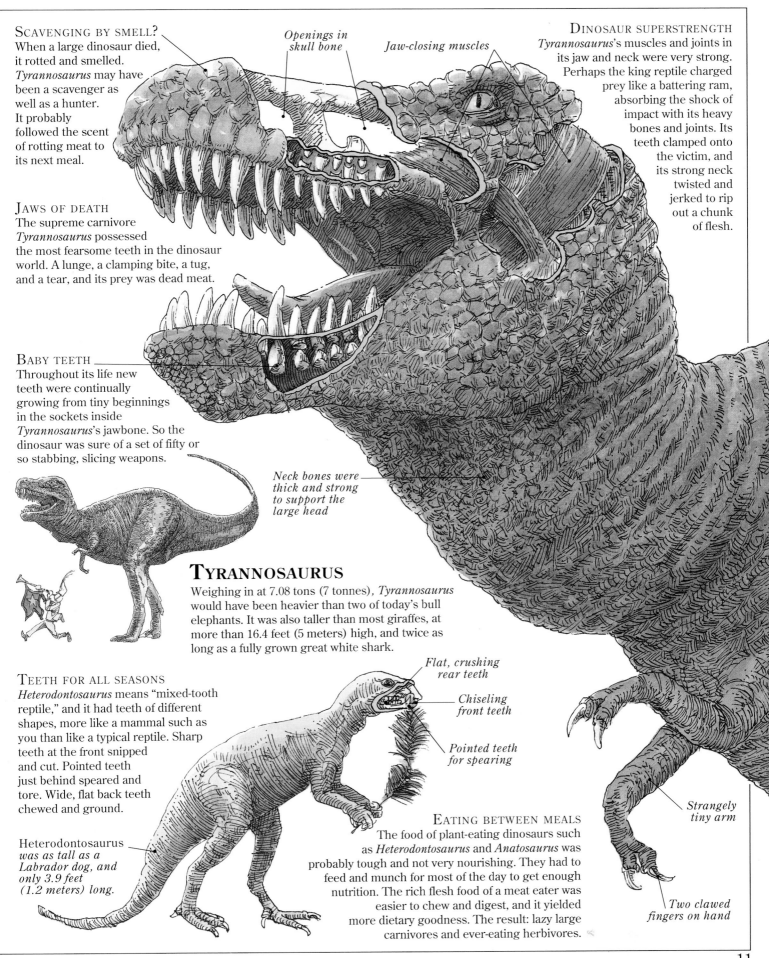

SCAVENGING BY SMELL?
When a large dinosaur died, it rotted and smelled. *Tyrannosaurus* may have been a scavenger as well as a hunter. It probably followed the scent of rotting meat to its next meal.

Openings in skull bone

Jaw-closing muscles

DINOSAUR SUPERSTRENGTH
Tyrannosaurus's muscles and joints in its jaw and neck were very strong. Perhaps the king reptile charged prey like a battering ram, absorbing the shock of impact with its heavy bones and joints. Its teeth clamped onto the victim, and its strong neck twisted and jerked to rip out a chunk of flesh.

JAWS OF DEATH
The supreme carnivore *Tyrannosaurus* possessed the most fearsome teeth in the dinosaur world. A lunge, a clamping bite, a tug, and a tear, and its prey was dead meat.

BABY TEETH
Throughout its life new teeth were continually growing from tiny beginnings in the sockets inside *Tyrannosaurus*'s jawbone. So the dinosaur was sure of a set of fifty or so stabbing, slicing weapons.

Neck bones were thick and strong to support the large head

TYRANNOSAURUS

Weighing in at 7.08 tons (7 tonnes), *Tyrannosaurus* would have been heavier than two of today's bull elephants. It was also taller than most giraffes, at more than 16.4 feet (5 meters) high, and twice as long as a fully grown great white shark.

TEETH FOR ALL SEASONS
Heterodontosaurus means "mixed-tooth reptile," and it had teeth of different shapes, more like a mammal such as you than like a typical reptile. Sharp teeth at the front snipped and cut. Pointed teeth just behind speared and tore. Wide, flat back teeth chewed and ground.

Heterodontosaurus *was as tall as a Labrador dog, and only 3.9 feet (1.2 meters) long.*

Flat, crushing rear teeth

Chiseling front teeth

Pointed teeth for spearing

EATING BETWEEN MEALS
The food of plant-eating dinosaurs such as *Heterodontosaurus* and *Anatosaurus* was probably tough and not very nourishing. They had to feed and munch for most of the day to get enough nutrition. The rich flesh food of a meat eater was easier to chew and digest, and it yielded more dietary goodness. The result: lazy large carnivores and ever-eating herbivores.

Strangely tiny arm

Two clawed fingers on hand

11

NECK AND NECK

THE FAMOUS SWAN'S NECK has nothing on the immensely long, snaking necks of some dinosaurs. Members of the sauropod group, such as *Diplodocus* and *Apatosaurus*, were the champion stretched necks. But why did the process of evolution come up with such a bizarre body plan? Standing in one spot, *Diplodocus* could sweep its head in an arc almost 65.6 feet (20 meters) across, saving energy while stripping the surrounding low vegetation of nourishment. That done, it could stretch up and reach plant food 16 to 19 feet (5 to 6 meters) above the ground, all without shifting its immense bulk. After craning its neck to look and sniff for predators and other dangers, the giant dinosaur would lumber on to the next vegetable patch.

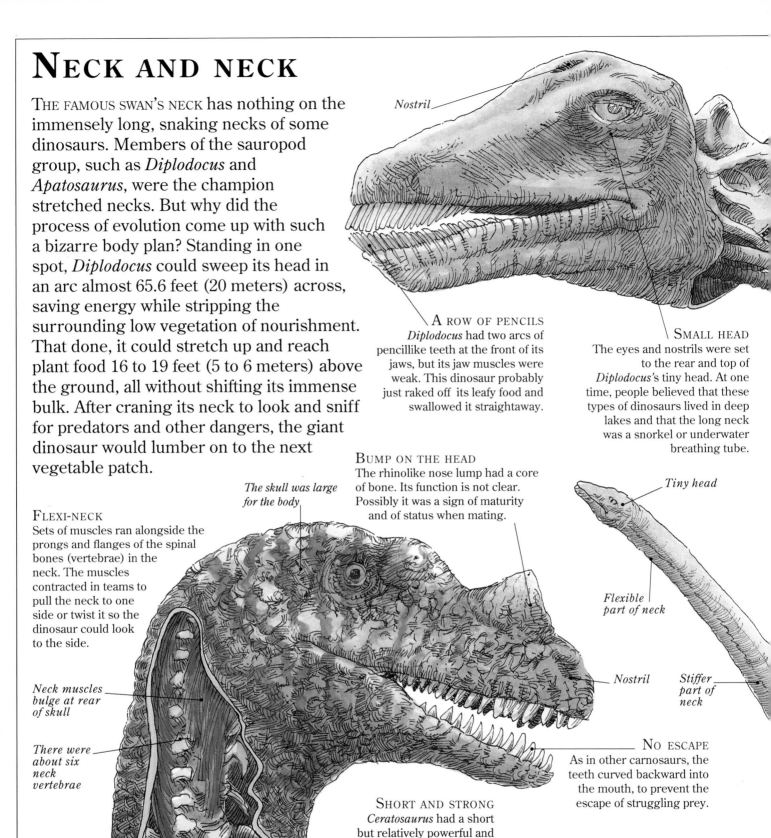

Nostril

A ROW OF PENCILS
Diplodocus had two arcs of pencillike teeth at the front of its jaws, but its jaw muscles were weak. This dinosaur probably just raked off its leafy food and swallowed it straightaway.

SMALL HEAD
The eyes and nostrils were set to the rear and top of *Diplodocus*'s tiny head. At one time, people believed that these types of dinosaurs lived in deep lakes and that the long neck was a snorkel or underwater breathing tube.

BUMP ON THE HEAD
The rhinolike nose lump had a core of bone. Its function is not clear. Possibly it was a sign of maturity and of status when mating.

The skull was large for the body

Tiny head

FLEXI-NECK
Sets of muscles ran alongside the prongs and flanges of the spinal bones (vertebrae) in the neck. The muscles contracted in teams to pull the neck to one side or twist it so the dinosaur could look to the side.

Flexible part of neck

Neck muscles bulge at rear of skull

There were about six neck vertebrae

Nostril

Stiffer part of neck

NO ESCAPE
As in other carnosaurs, the teeth curved backward into the mouth, to prevent the escape of struggling prey.

Muscles alongside chest vertebrae

SHORT AND STRONG
Ceratosaurus had a short but relatively powerful and flexible neck. It may have swung its head to snap at victims and tug off pieces of flesh by a twisting and sawing motion.

CARNIVORE COUSINS
The "horned reptile" *Ceratosaurus* is named from the bump on its nose. It was some 19.6 feet (6 meters) long and stood 8.2 feet (2.5 meters) high. Fossils indicate that it was a meat-eating relative of the better-known *Allosaurus*. It stalked western North America during the late Jurassic period, about 150 million years ago.

Rib

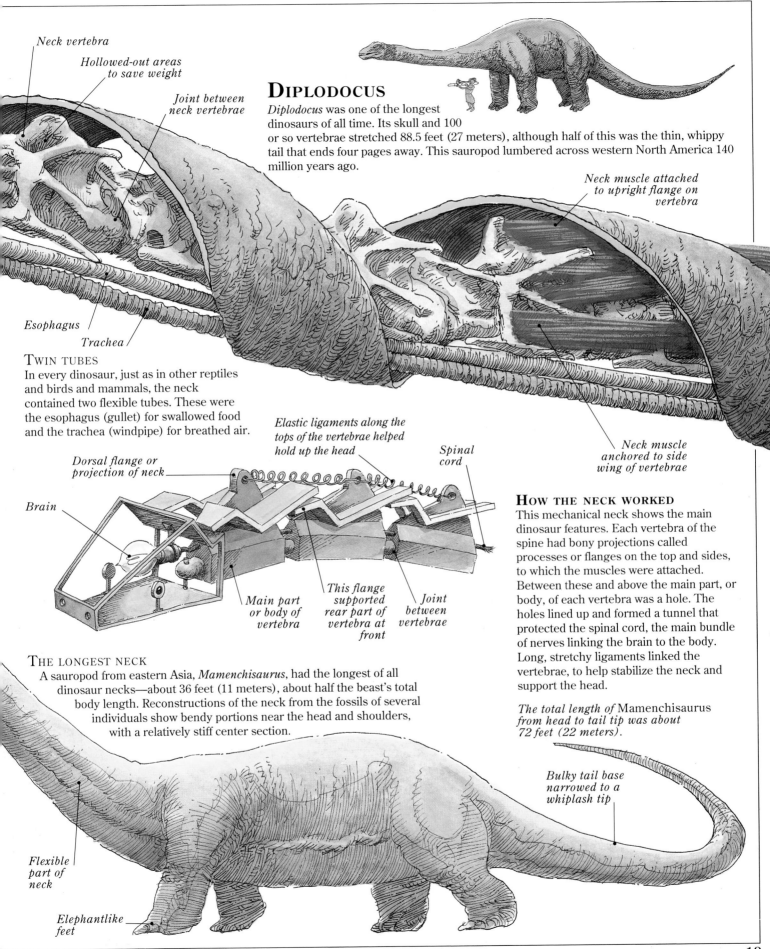

Neck vertebra

Hollowed-out areas
to save weight

Joint between
neck vertebrae

DIPLODOCUS

Diplodocus was one of the longest
dinosaurs of all time. Its skull and 100
or so vertebrae stretched 88.5 feet (27 meters), although half of this was the thin, whippy
tail that ends four pages away. This sauropod lumbered across western North America 140
million years ago.

Neck muscle attached
to upright flange on
vertebra

Esophagus

Trachea

TWIN TUBES

In every dinosaur, just as in other reptiles
and birds and mammals, the neck
contained two flexible tubes. These were
the esophagus (gullet) for swallowed food
and the trachea (windpipe) for breathed air.

Neck muscle
anchored to side
wing of vertebrae

*Elastic ligaments along the
tops of the vertebrae helped
hold up the head*

Spinal
cord

Dorsal flange or
projection of neck

Brain

HOW THE NECK WORKED

This mechanical neck shows the main
dinosaur features. Each vertebra of the
spine had bony projections called
processes or flanges on the top and sides,
to which the muscles were attached.
Between these and above the main part, or
body, of each vertebra was a hole. The
holes lined up and formed a tunnel that
protected the spinal cord, the main bundle
of nerves linking the brain to the body.
Long, stretchy ligaments linked the
vertebrae, to help stabilize the neck and
support the head.

Main part
or body of
vertebra

*This flange
supported
rear part of
vertebra at
front*

Joint
between
vertebrae

THE LONGEST NECK

A sauropod from eastern Asia, *Mamenchisaurus*, had the longest of all
dinosaur necks—about 36 feet (11 meters), about half the beast's total
body length. Reconstructions of the neck from the fossils of several
individuals show bendy portions near the head and shoulders,
with a relatively stiff center section.

The total length of Mamenchisaurus
*from head to tail tip was about
72 feet (22 meters).*

Bulky tail base
narrowed to a
whiplash tip

Flexible
part of
neck

Elephantlike
feet

ON ALL FOURS

IF YOU ARE AN AVERAGE TEN-YEAR-OLD (and who isn't at heart?), each of your feet supports about 33 pounds (15 kilograms). Each of *Diplodocus*'s feet carried two hundred times as much weight! But the dinosaur was rock steady on them, since its head and neck (on the previous two pages) counterbalanced its tail (on the next three pages)

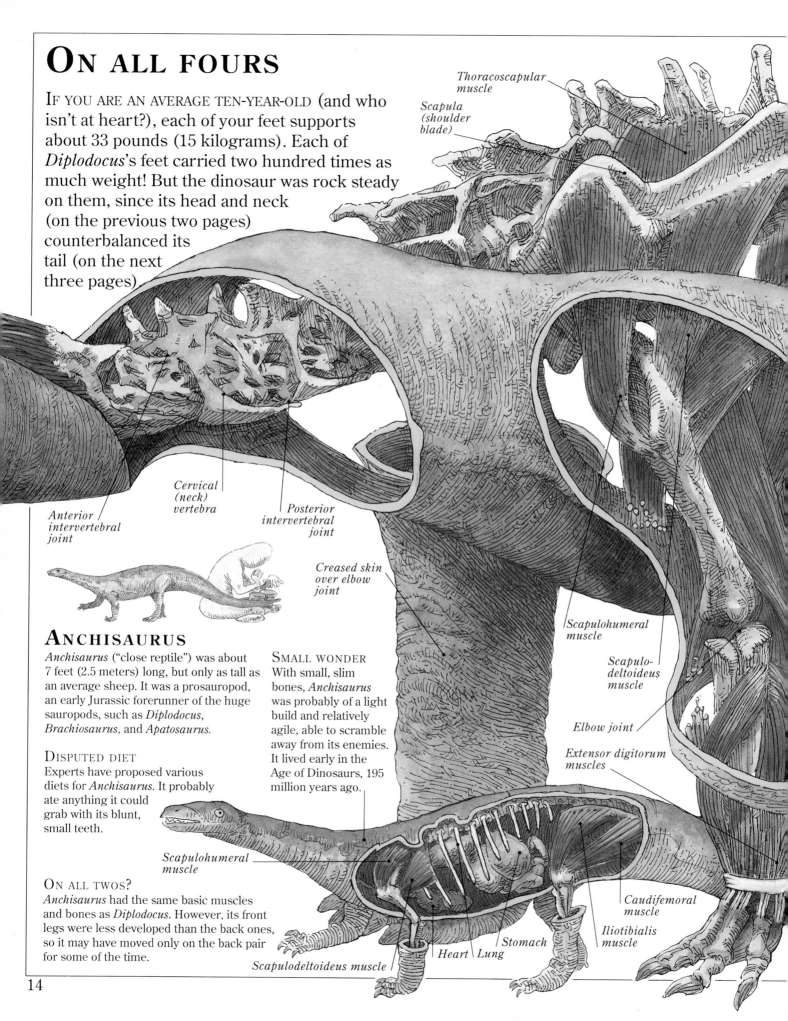

Thoracoscapular muscle

Scapula (shoulder blade)

Anterior intervertebral joint

Cervical (neck) vertebra

Posterior intervertebral joint

Creased skin over elbow joint

Scapulohumeral muscle

Scapulo-deltoideus muscle

Elbow joint

Extensor digitorum muscles

ANCHISAURUS

Anchisaurus ("close reptile") was about 7 feet (2.5 meters) long, but only as tall as an average sheep. It was a prosauropod, an early Jurassic forerunner of the huge sauropods, such as *Diplodocus*, *Brachiosaurus*, and *Apatosaurus*.

DISPUTED DIET
Experts have proposed various diets for *Anchisaurus*. It probably ate anything it could grab with its blunt, small teeth.

SMALL WONDER
With small, slim bones, *Anchisaurus* was probably of a light build and relatively agile, able to scramble away from its enemies. It lived early in the Age of Dinosaurs, 195 million years ago.

Scapulohumeral muscle

ON ALL TWOS?
Anchisaurus had the same basic muscles and bones as *Diplodocus*. However, its front legs were less developed than the back ones, so it may have moved only on the back pair for some of the time.

Scapulodeltoideus muscle

Heart Lung Stomach

Caudifemoral muscle

Iliotibialis muscle

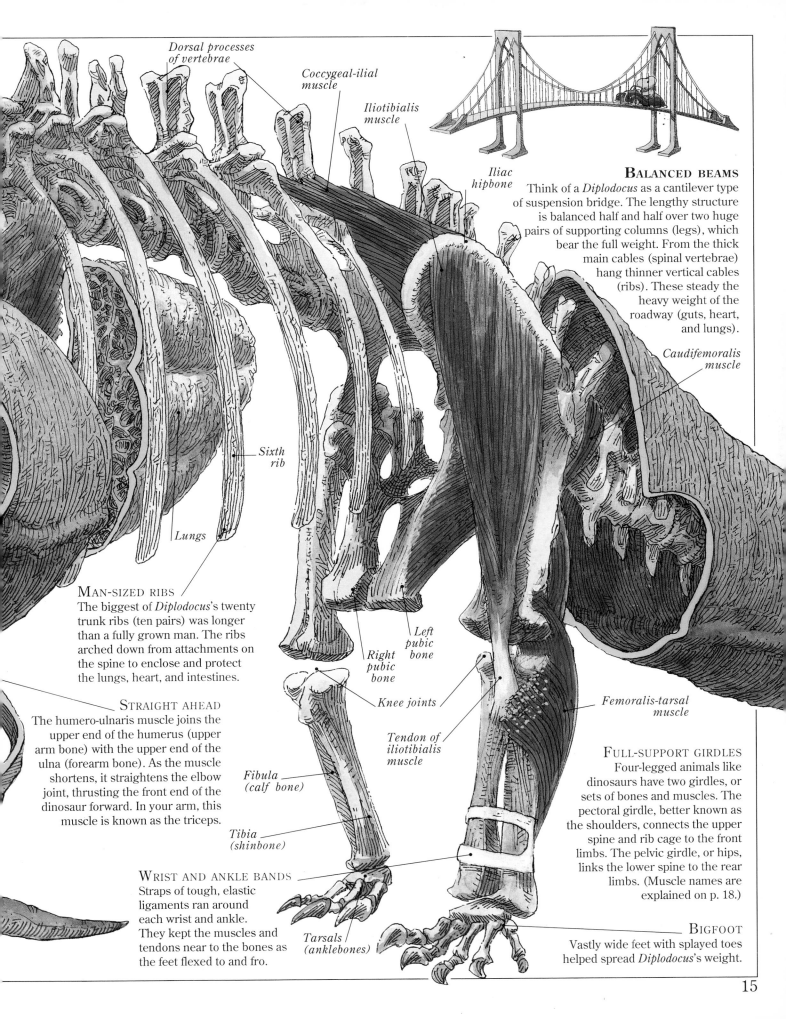

*Dorsal processes
of vertebrae*

*Coccygeal-ilial
muscle*

*Iliotibialis
muscle*

*Iliac
hipbone*

BALANCED BEAMS
Think of a *Diplodocus* as a cantilever type
of suspension bridge. The lengthy structure
is balanced half and half over two huge
pairs of supporting columns (legs), which
bear the full weight. From the thick
main cables (spinal vertebrae)
hang thinner vertical cables
(ribs). These steady the
heavy weight of the
roadway (guts, heart,
and lungs).

*Caudifemoralis
muscle*

*Sixth
rib*

Lungs

MAN-SIZED RIBS
The biggest of *Diplodocus*'s twenty
trunk ribs (ten pairs) was longer
than a fully grown man. The ribs
arched down from attachments on
the spine to enclose and protect
the lungs, heart, and intestines.

STRAIGHT AHEAD
The humero-ulnaris muscle joins the
upper end of the humerus (upper
arm bone) with the upper end of the
ulna (forearm bone). As the muscle
shortens, it straightens the elbow
joint, thrusting the front end of the
dinosaur forward. In your arm, this
muscle is known as the triceps.

*Left
pubic
bone*

*Right
pubic
bone*

Knee joints

*Tendon of
iliotibialis
muscle*

*Femoralis-tarsal
muscle*

FULL-SUPPORT GIRDLES
Four-legged animals like
dinosaurs have two girdles, or
sets of bones and muscles. The
pectoral girdle, better known as
the shoulders, connects the upper
spine and rib cage to the front
limbs. The pelvic girdle, or hips,
links the lower spine to the rear
limbs. (Muscle names are
explained on p. 18.)

*Fibula
(calf bone)*

*Tibia
(shinbone)*

WRIST AND ANKLE BANDS
Straps of tough, elastic
ligaments ran around
each wrist and ankle.
They kept the muscles and
tendons near to the bones as
the feet flexed to and fro.

*Tarsals
(anklebones)*

BIGFOOT
Vastly wide feet with splayed toes
helped spread *Diplodocus*'s weight.

15

TAIL-ENDERS

Dinosaur tails did more than just trail along behind their owners. They were long whips, spiky maces, muscle anchors, adjustable counterweights, steering rudders, or, in the case of *Euoplocephalus*, heavy clubs capable of delivering a knockout blow. The dinosaurs shown here were all plant eaters. They lacked the large, sharp teeth and claws of the carnivores, which doubled as both feeding utensils and defensive weapons. Self-defense gadgets evolved at the other end of their bodies.

An array of armor
Euoplocephalus sported a formidable array of spikes, spines, shields, and plates. It must have been an awkward mouthful for its tyrannosaur predators. As you might expect from a dinosaur whose name means "true plated head," even the eyelids were armored.

Beak and teeth
With a broad, toothless beak at the front of its jaws and small, weak cheek teeth, *Euoplocephalus* probably fed on soft, easy-to-chew vegetation.

Mr. whippy
The vertebrae midway along *Diplodocus*'s tail had sideways and dorsal (upper) processes to anchor muscles. The joints between the vertebrae were relatively flexible, so *Diplodocus* could whip the tip of its tail at will, wielding it as an effective lash. Perhaps it cracked its tail like a ringmaster, frightening away enemies with the sound.

Sharp, spiky rear spears
Stegosaurus (see p. 26) had two pointy pairs of bone-cored tail spikes. Together, they formed a fierce, macelike weapon, which was swung from side to side to puncture a predator.

Larger spike was more than twenty-three inches (60 cm) long

Base embedded in skin

Paired large dorsal spines

Temple spike

Shoulder spear

Neck shield

Shoulder nodule

Bony eyelid plate

Cheek spine

Bony lumps on forearm

Tough, leathery skin

Iliotibialis muscles

Wrist joint

Elbow joint

Clawed front foot

Dorsal intervertebral muscles

Dorsal process

Transverse intervertebral muscles

Transverse (side) process

Intervertebral joint

Dorsal and transverse processes anchored muscles

Tapering vertebrae

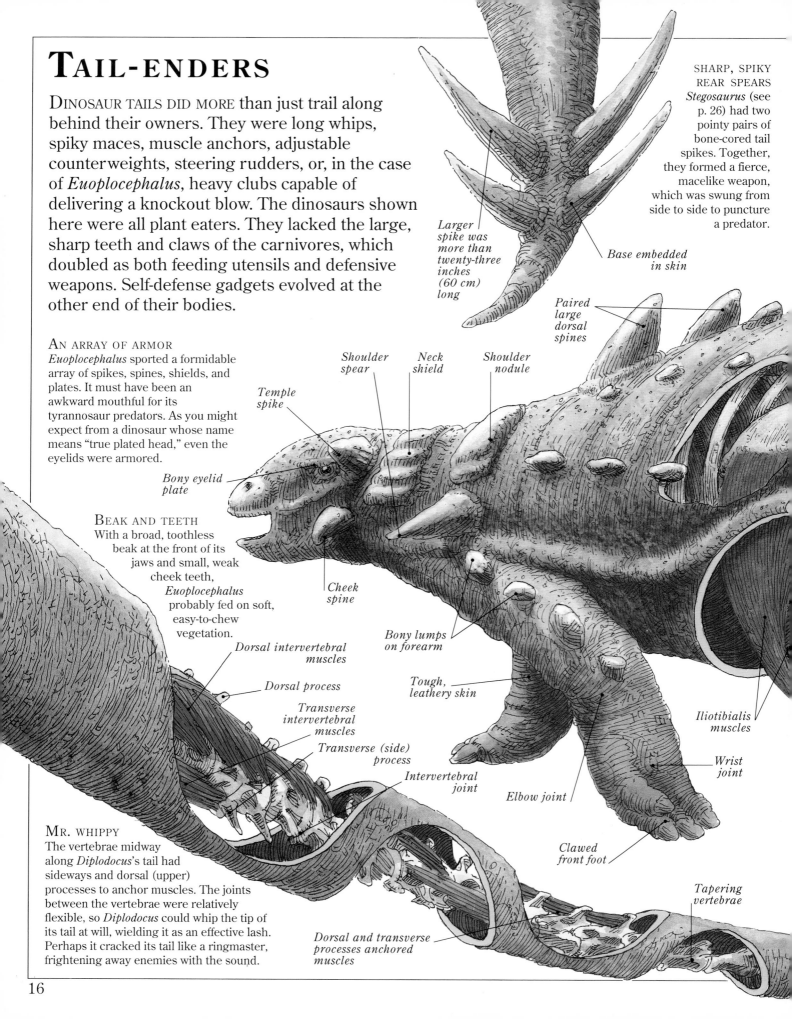

EUOPLOCEPHALUS

This medium-size ankylosaur was about the size of a school minibus: 19.6 feet (6 meters) long, just taller than an adult, and 2.4 tons (2 tonnes) in weight. As dinosaurs go, it is fairly well known, from eighty-million-year-old fossils unearthed in Alberta, Canada.

TAILING OFF THE PAGE
Below is *Pachycephalosaurus*'s shortish, stiffish tail. The rest of this two-legged "head butter" has charged over to the next page. The dinosaur used its tail chiefly as a counterbalance as it sprinted along with its body held horizontal.

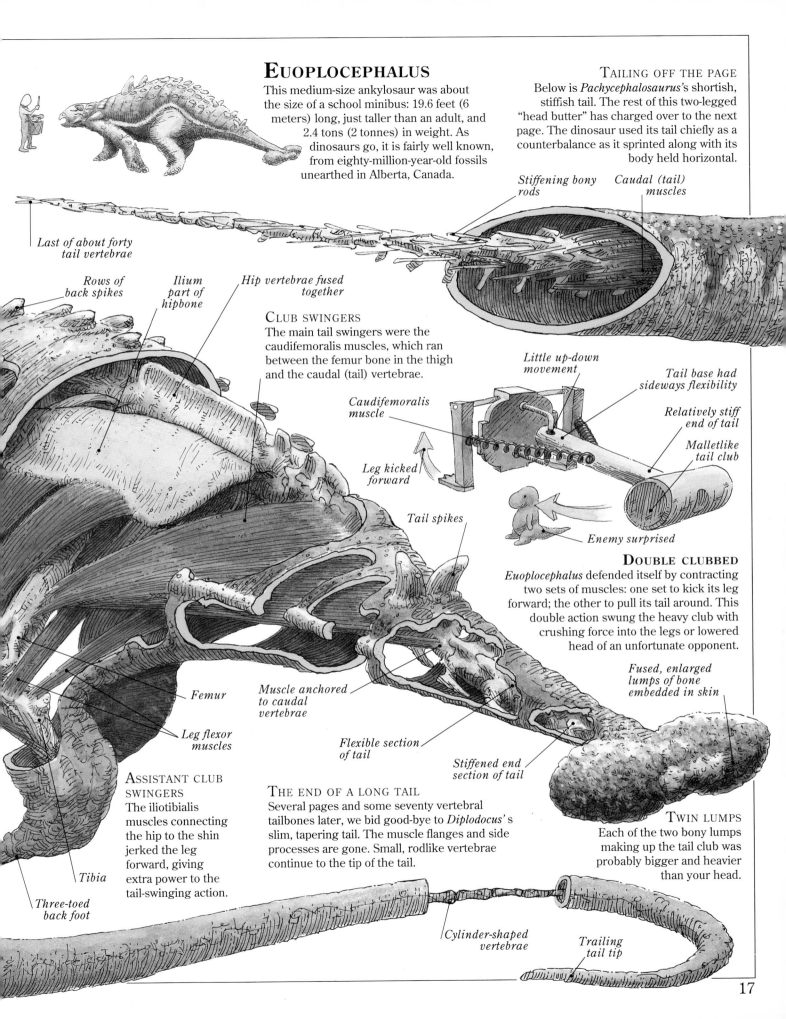

Stiffening bony rods

Caudal (tail) muscles

Last of about forty tail vertebrae

Rows of back spikes

Ilium part of hipbone

Hip vertebrae fused together

CLUB SWINGERS
The main tail swingers were the caudifemoralis muscles, which ran between the femur bone in the thigh and the caudal (tail) vertebrae.

Little up-down movement

Caudifemoralis muscle

Tail base had sideways flexibility

Relatively stiff end of tail

Malletlike tail club

Leg kicked forward

Enemy surprised

Tail spikes

DOUBLE CLUBBED
Euoplocephalus defended itself by contracting two sets of muscles: one set to kick its leg forward; the other to pull its tail around. This double action swung the heavy club with crushing force into the legs or lowered head of an unfortunate opponent.

Femur

Muscle anchored to caudal vertebrae

Flexible section of tail

Stiffened end section of tail

Fused, enlarged lumps of bone embedded in skin

Leg flexor muscles

ASSISTANT CLUB SWINGERS
The iliotibialis muscles connecting the hip to the shin jerked the leg forward, giving extra power to the tail-swinging action.

THE END OF A LONG TAIL
Several pages and some seventy vertebral tailbones later, we bid good-bye to *Diplodocus*'s slim, tapering tail. The muscle flanges and side processes are gone. Small, rodlike vertebrae continue to the tip of the tail.

TWIN LUMPS
Each of the two bony lumps making up the tail club was probably bigger and heavier than your head.

Tibia

Three-toed back foot

Cylinder-shaped vertebrae

Trailing tail tip

UP AND RUNNING

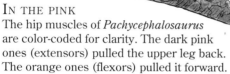

HEAD DOWN, NECK STRAIGHT OUT IN FRONT, tail stiff behind, body well balanced over muscular back legs, *Pachycephalosaurus* prepares to charge at a rival in the mating game. Many two-legged dinosaurs were slim and long-limbed, a sure sign of speed all those millions of years ago, just as it is in today's racehorses and ostriches.

ROD-RIGID
Small bony rods linked the vertebrae of the backbone and helped stiffen it in the back and hip area.

Hip joint

Rear ribs

Ilium (main part of hipbone)

IN THE PINK
The hip muscles of *Pachycephalosaurus* are color-coded for clarity. The dark pink ones (extensors) pulled the upper leg back. The orange ones (flexors) pulled it forward.

Muscle connecting tail to femur (thighbone)

Muscles connecting ischium (hipbone) to femur (thighbone)

Tail

Head and neck

Muscle connecting tail to tibia (shin)

Right femur (thighbone)

Right knee joint

KNEES UP
The iliotibialis muscle joined the ilial part of the hipbone to the shin, or tibia, to raise the knee.

Rear leg under body's center of gravity

Muscles connecting tibia (shin) to tarsus (ankle)

Stiffened tail tip

BALANCING THE BODY
Some older reconstructions of two-legged dinosaurs show them running in an upright position, chest and neck vertical. This would have been very tiring. It is more likely that the dinosaur tipped head and neck forward so that the body's weight was centered over the rear legs. At rest the body would tilt more upright, so the dinosaur could scan and sniff for danger.

MUSCLES
Dinosaurs, like humans, had several hundred body muscles. One common system for identifying them is to combine the names of the bones to which they were attached at each end. For example, the tibialis-tarsus pulled on the tibia (shin) and tarsus (ankle) to tip the toes down.

Shaft of tibia (shinbone)

Skin covered ankle

First toe was a short "spur"

Three clawed toes

Metatarsals (foot bones)

Metatarsal bones (main part of foot) under skin

Knuckles (toe joints)

Phalanges (toe bones)

THIRD LEVER
Compared with a plodder such as *Diplodocus*, the *Pachycephalosaurus* had long, slim foot bones. Like the thigh and shin, the foot was a lever to increase running efficiency.

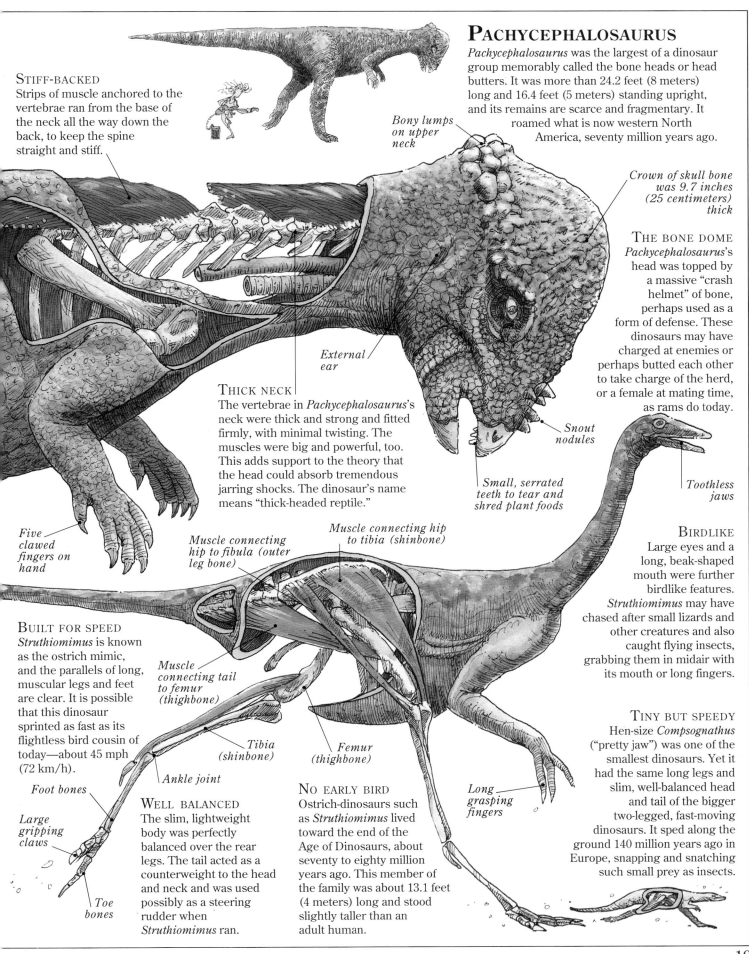

PACHYCEPHALOSAURUS

Pachycephalosaurus was the largest of a dinosaur group memorably called the bone heads or head butters. It was more than 24.2 feet (8 meters) long and 16.4 feet (5 meters) standing upright, and its remains are scarce and fragmentary. It roamed what is now western North America, seventy million years ago.

STIFF-BACKED
Strips of muscle anchored to the vertebrae ran from the base of the neck all the way down the back, to keep the spine straight and stiff.

Bony lumps on upper neck

Crown of skull bone was 9.7 inches (25 centimeters) thick

THE BONE DOME
Pachycephalosaurus's head was topped by a massive "crash helmet" of bone, perhaps used as a form of defense. These dinosaurs may have charged at enemies or perhaps butted each other to take charge of the herd, or a female at mating time, as rams do today.

External ear

THICK NECK
The vertebrae in *Pachycephalosaurus*'s neck were thick and strong and fitted firmly, with minimal twisting. The muscles were big and powerful, too. This adds support to the theory that the head could absorb tremendous jarring shocks. The dinosaur's name means "thick-headed reptile."

Snout nodules

Small, serrated teeth to tear and shred plant foods

Toothless jaws

Five clawed fingers on hand

Muscle connecting hip to fibula (outer leg bone)

Muscle connecting hip to tibia (shinbone)

BIRDLIKE
Large eyes and a long, beak-shaped mouth were further birdlike features. *Struthiomimus* may have chased after small lizards and other creatures and also caught flying insects, grabbing them in midair with its mouth or long fingers.

BUILT FOR SPEED
Struthiomimus is known as the ostrich mimic, and the parallels of long, muscular legs and feet are clear. It is possible that this dinosaur sprinted as fast as its flightless bird cousin of today—about 45 mph (72 km/h).

Muscle connecting tail to femur (thighbone)

Tibia (shinbone)

Femur (thighbone)

Ankle joint

Long grasping fingers

Foot bones

Large gripping claws

WELL BALANCED
The slim, lightweight body was perfectly balanced over the rear legs. The tail acted as a counterweight to the head and neck and was used possibly as a steering rudder when *Struthiomimus* ran.

Toe bones

NO EARLY BIRD
Ostrich-dinosaurs such as *Struthiomimus* lived toward the end of the Age of Dinosaurs, about seventy to eighty million years ago. This member of the family was about 13.1 feet (4 meters) long and stood slightly taller than an adult human.

TINY BUT SPEEDY
Hen-size *Compsognathus* ("pretty jaw") was one of the smallest dinosaurs. Yet it had the same long legs and slim, well-balanced head and tail of the bigger two-legged, fast-moving dinosaurs. It sped along the ground 140 million years ago in Europe, snapping and snatching such small prey as insects.

SLASH AND GNASH

SOME DINOSAURS LIVED BY feeding on others; it was a dinosaur-eat-dinosaur world. Clues in its fossilized remains tell you if a dinosaur was a hunter or the hunted. Sharp teeth and pointy claws denote both the hunting weapons and the defensive tools of the predator. A fine dinosaur example was the pack-hunting, human-size "terrible claw" *Deinonychus*. Its sharp, daggerlike claw on each foot could slash, maim, and dismember a victim with one deadly swipe.

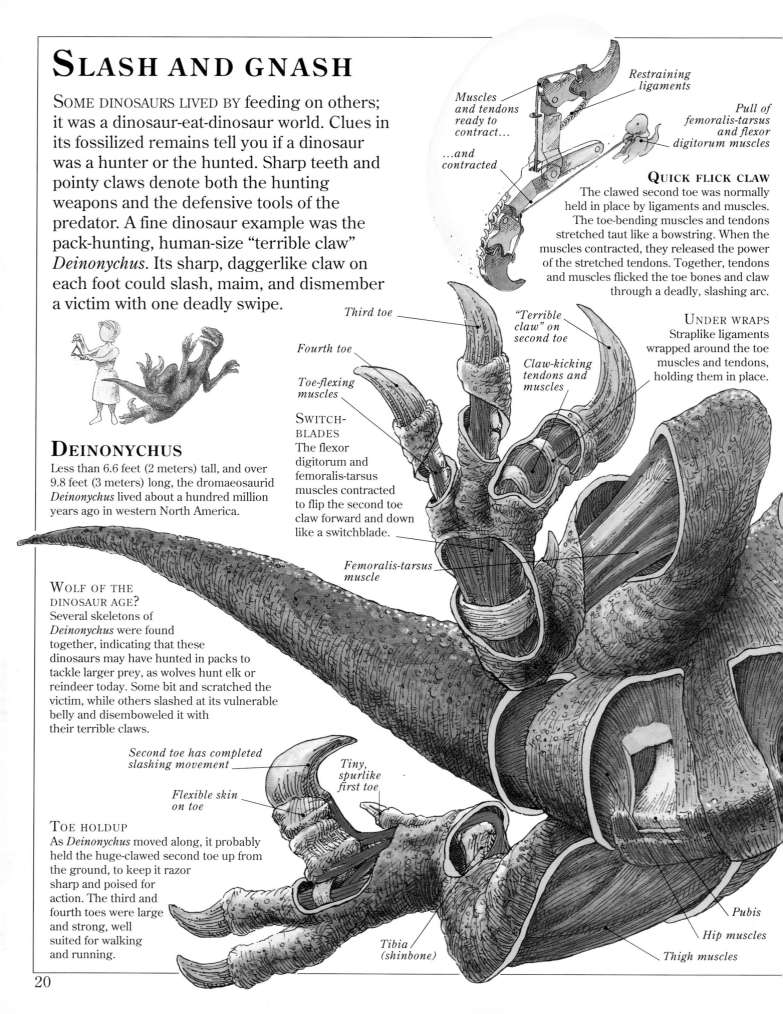

QUICK FLICK CLAW
The clawed second toe was normally held in place by ligaments and muscles. The toe-bending muscles and tendons stretched taut like a bowstring. When the muscles contracted, they released the power of the stretched tendons. Together, tendons and muscles flicked the toe bones and claw through a deadly, slashing arc.

Muscles and tendons ready to contract...
...and contracted

Restraining ligaments

Pull of femoralis-tarsus and flexor digitorum muscles

UNDER WRAPS
Straplike ligaments wrapped around the toe muscles and tendons, holding them in place.

Third toe

Fourth toe

"Terrible claw" on second toe

Claw-kicking tendons and muscles

Toe-flexing muscles

SWITCH-BLADES
The flexor digitorum and femoralis-tarsus muscles contracted to flip the second toe claw forward and down like a switchblade.

Femoralis-tarsus muscle

DEINONYCHUS

Less than 6.6 feet (2 meters) tall, and over 9.8 feet (3 meters) long, the dromaeosaurid *Deinonychus* lived about a hundred million years ago in western North America.

WOLF OF THE DINOSAUR AGE?
Several skeletons of *Deinonychus* were found together, indicating that these dinosaurs may have hunted in packs to tackle larger prey, as wolves hunt elk or reindeer today. Some bit and scratched the victim, while others slashed at its vulnerable belly and disemboweled it with their terrible claws.

Second toe has completed slashing movement

Flexible skin on toe

Tiny, spurlike first toe

TOE HOLDUP
As *Deinonychus* moved along, it probably held the huge-clawed second toe up from the ground, to keep it razor sharp and poised for action. The third and fourth toes were large and strong, well suited for walking and running.

Pubis

Hip muscles

Thigh muscles

Tibia (shinbone)

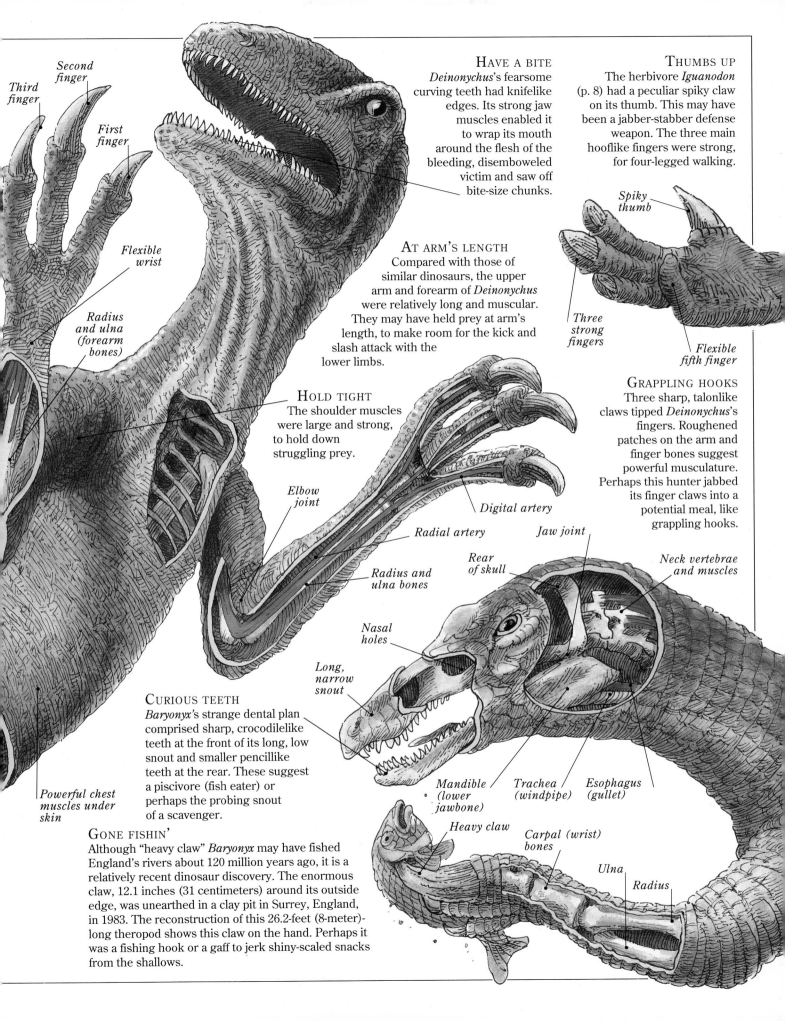

Third finger

Second finger

First finger

Flexible wrist

Radius and ulna (forearm bones)

HAVE A BITE
Deinonychus's fearsome curving teeth had knifelike edges. Its strong jaw muscles enabled it to wrap its mouth around the flesh of the bleeding, disemboweled victim and saw off bite-size chunks.

THUMBS UP
The herbivore *Iguanodon* (p. 8) had a peculiar spiky claw on its thumb. This may have been a jabber-stabber defense weapon. The three main hooflike fingers were strong, for four-legged walking.

Spiky thumb

Three strong fingers

Flexible fifth finger

AT ARM'S LENGTH
Compared with those of similar dinosaurs, the upper arm and forearm of *Deinonychus* were relatively long and muscular. They may have held prey at arm's length, to make room for the kick and slash attack with the lower limbs.

GRAPPLING HOOKS
Three sharp, talonlike claws tipped *Deinonychus*'s fingers. Roughened patches on the arm and finger bones suggest powerful musculature. Perhaps this hunter jabbed its finger claws into a potential meal, like grappling hooks.

HOLD TIGHT
The shoulder muscles were large and strong, to hold down struggling prey.

Elbow joint

Digital artery

Radial artery

Jaw joint

Rear of skull

Neck vertebrae and muscles

Radius and ulna bones

Nasal holes

Long, narrow snout

CURIOUS TEETH
Baryonyx's strange dental plan comprised sharp, crocodilelike teeth at the front of its long, low snout and smaller pencillike teeth at the rear. These suggest a piscivore (fish eater) or perhaps the probing snout of a scavenger.

Mandible (lower jawbone)

Trachea (windpipe)

Esophagus (gullet)

Heavy claw

Carpal (wrist) bones

Ulna

Radius

Powerful chest muscles under skin

GONE FISHIN'
Although "heavy claw" *Baryonyx* may have fished England's rivers about 120 million years ago, it is a relatively recent dinosaur discovery. The enormous claw, 12.1 inches (31 centimeters) around its outside edge, was unearthed in a clay pit in Surrey, England, in 1983. The reconstruction of this 26.2-feet (8-meter)-long theropod shows this claw on the hand. Perhaps it was a fishing hook or a gaff to jerk shiny-scaled snacks from the shallows.

ARMORED AND DANGEROUS

MEDIEVAL KNIGHTS IN ARMOR were mere amateurs compared to the ankylosaurs, the "fused reptile" dinosaurs. The name refers to the way horny scales and plates of bone evolved and joined together to protect almost every part of their anatomy, except the ever-vulnerable belly. One subgroup, the ankylosaurids, included *Euoplocephalus* (see p. 16). The other ankylosaur subgroup were the nodosaurids, such as *Hylaeosaurus*, shown here. This tanklike reptile could have frightened away those who wanted to make a meal of it simply by squatting down on the ground and looking scary. Running away was probably out of the question. Ankylosaur armor was so thick that few predators could break through, but so heavy that it may have prevented a quick getaway.

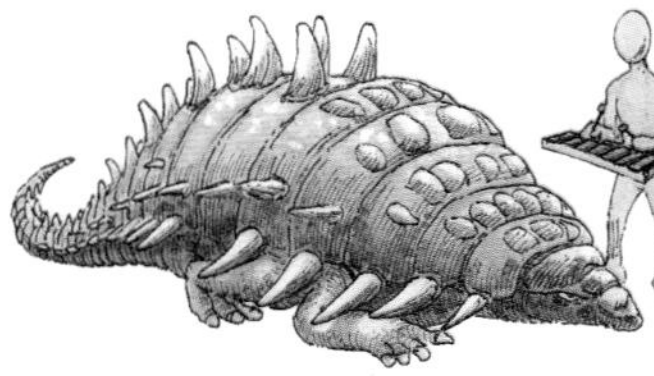

HYLAEOSAURUS
Thirteen feet (4 meters) long, and twenty times the weight of a human, this squat beast was one of the original *Dinosauria* named by Richard Owen in 1841. It lived 130 million years ago in southern England and northern France. The name means "woodland reptile"— some of its fossils were found in a forest.

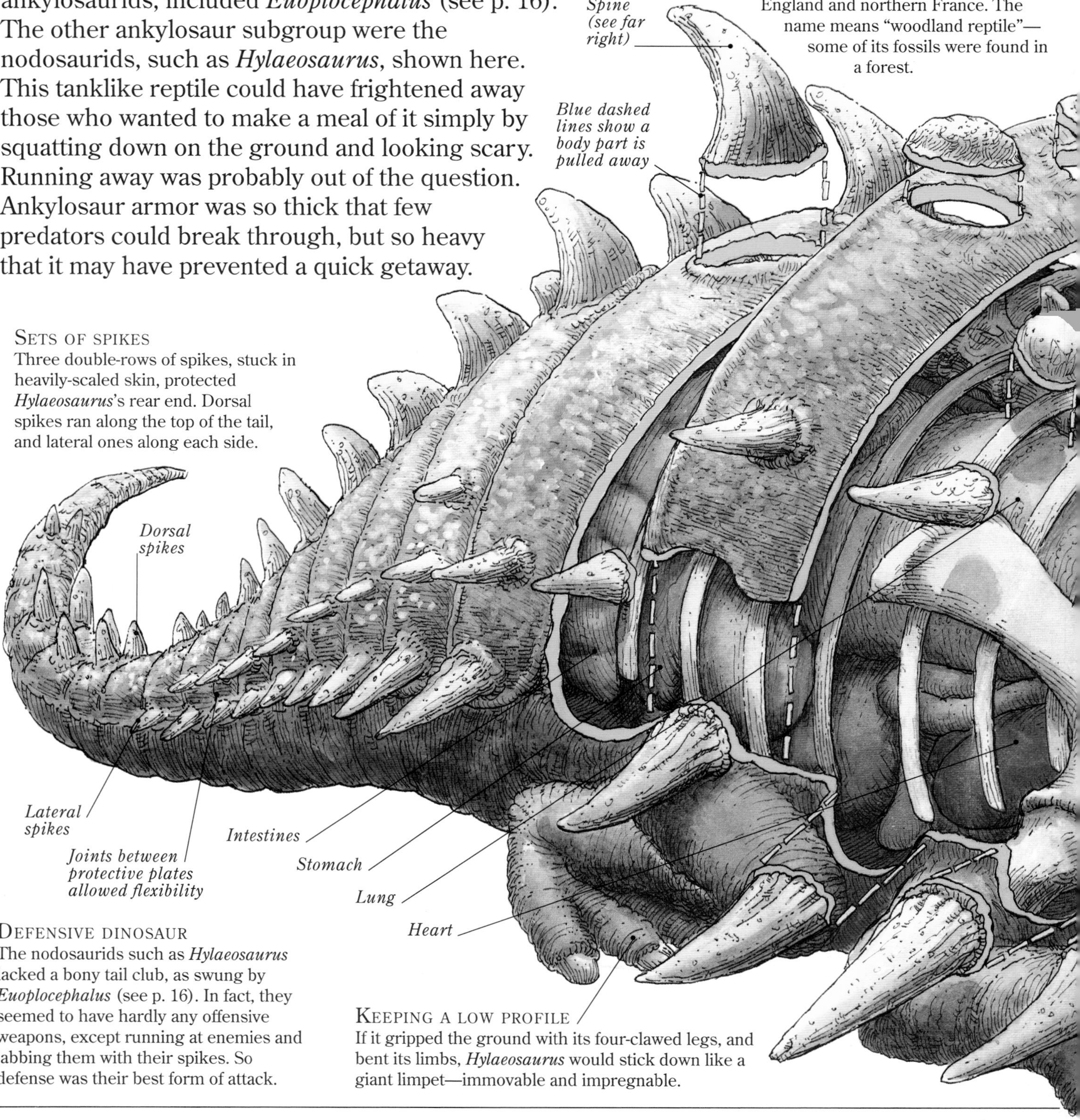

Spine (see far right)

Blue dashed lines show a body part is pulled away

SETS OF SPIKES
Three double-rows of spikes, stuck in heavily-scaled skin, protected *Hylaeosaurus*'s rear end. Dorsal spikes ran along the top of the tail, and lateral ones along each side.

Dorsal spikes

Lateral spikes

Joints between protective plates allowed flexibility

Intestines

Stomach

Lung

Heart

DEFENSIVE DINOSAUR
The nodosaurids such as *Hylaeosaurus* lacked a bony tail club, as swung by *Euoplocephalus* (see p. 16). In fact, they seemed to have hardly any offensive weapons, except running at enemies and jabbing them with their spikes. So defense was their best form of attack.

KEEPING A LOW PROFILE
If it gripped the ground with its four-clawed legs, and bent its limbs, *Hylaeosaurus* would stick down like a giant limpet—immovable and impregnable.

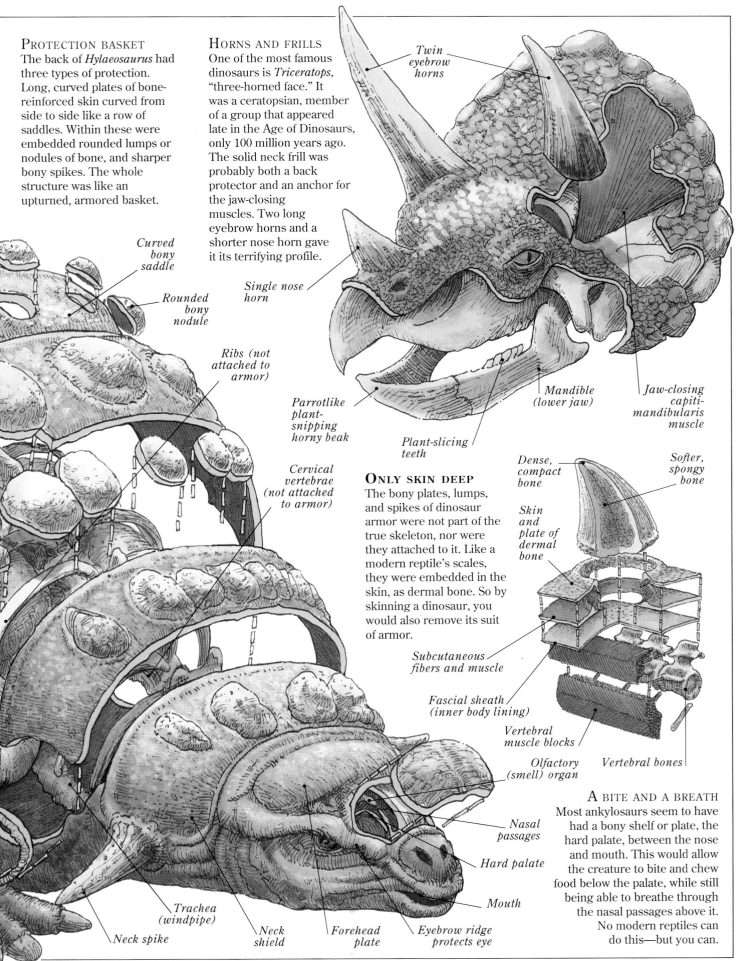

PROTECTION BASKET
The back of *Hylaeosaurus* had three types of protection. Long, curved plates of bone-reinforced skin curved from side to side like a row of saddles. Within these were embedded rounded lumps or nodules of bone, and sharper bony spikes. The whole structure was like an upturned, armored basket.

HORNS AND FRILLS
One of the most famous dinosaurs is *Triceratops*, "three-horned face." It was a ceratopsian, member of a group that appeared late in the Age of Dinosaurs, only 100 million years ago. The solid neck frill was probably both a back protector and an anchor for the jaw-closing muscles. Two long eyebrow horns and a shorter nose horn gave it its terrifying profile.

Twin eyebrow horns

Single nose horn

Curved bony saddle

Rounded bony nodule

Ribs (not attached to armor)

Parrotlike plant-snipping horny beak

Cervical vertebrae (not attached to armor)

Plant-slicing teeth

Mandible (lower jaw)

Jaw-closing capiti-mandibularis muscle

ONLY SKIN DEEP
The bony plates, lumps, and spikes of dinosaur armor were not part of the true skeleton, nor were they attached to it. Like a modern reptile's scales, they were embedded in the skin, as dermal bone. So by skinning a dinosaur, you would also remove its suit of armor.

Dense, compact bone

Softer, spongy bone

Skin and plate of dermal bone

Subcutaneous fibers and muscle

Fascial sheath (inner body lining)

Vertebral muscle blocks

Vertebral bones

Olfactory (smell) organ

Nasal passages

Hard palate

Mouth

Trachea (windpipe)

Neck spike

Neck shield

Forehead plate

Eyebrow ridge protects eye

A BITE AND A BREATH
Most ankylosaurs seem to have had a bony shelf or plate, the hard palate, between the nose and mouth. This would allow the creature to bite and chew food below the palate, while still being able to breathe through the nasal passages above it. No modern reptiles can do this—but you can.

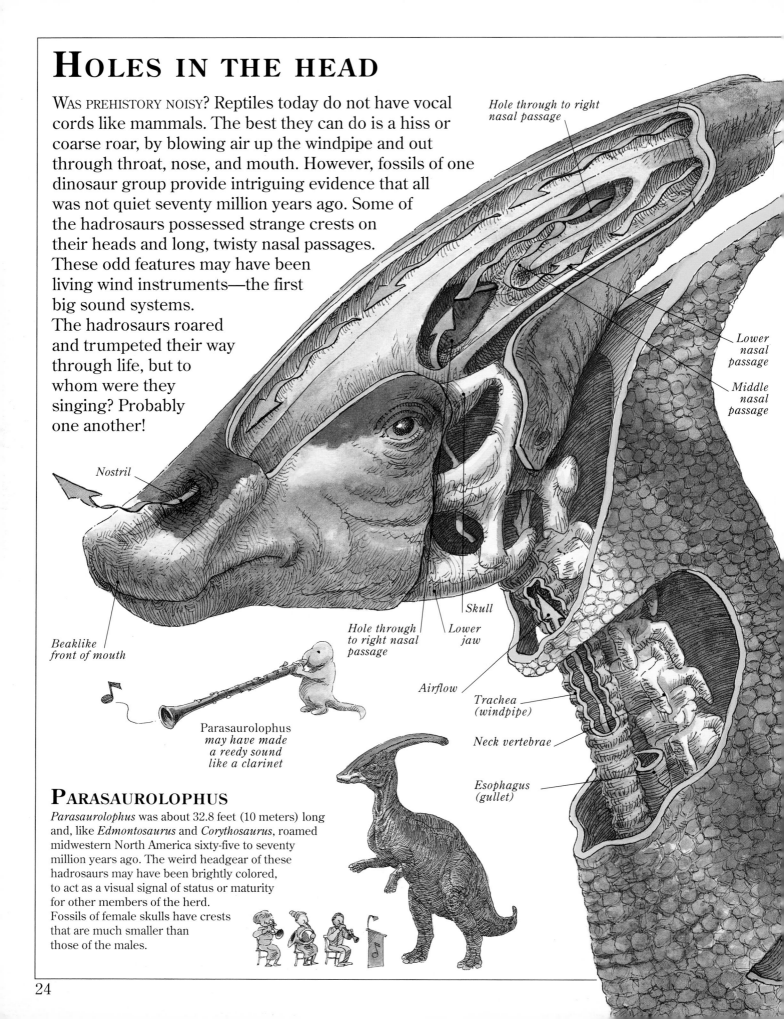

HOLES IN THE HEAD

WAS PREHISTORY NOISY? Reptiles today do not have vocal cords like mammals. The best they can do is a hiss or coarse roar, by blowing air up the windpipe and out through throat, nose, and mouth. However, fossils of one dinosaur group provide intriguing evidence that all was not quiet seventy million years ago. Some of the hadrosaurs possessed strange crests on their heads and long, twisty nasal passages. These odd features may have been living wind instruments—the first big sound systems. The hadrosaurs roared and trumpeted their way through life, but to whom were they singing? Probably one another!

Hole through to right nasal passage

Lower nasal passage

Middle nasal passage

Nostril

Beaklike front of mouth

Skull

Hole through to right nasal passage

Lower jaw

Airflow

Trachea (windpipe)

Neck vertebrae

Esophagus (gullet)

Parasaurolophus *may have made a reedy sound like a clarinet*

PARASAUROLOPHUS

Parasaurolophus was about 32.8 feet (10 meters) long and, like *Edmontosaurus* and *Corythosaurus*, roamed midwestern North America sixty-five to seventy million years ago. The weird headgear of these hadrosaurs may have been brightly colored, to act as a visual signal of status or maturity for other members of the herd. Fossils of female skulls have crests that are much smaller than those of the males.

Nasal passages

WIND INSTRUMENT
Parasaurolophus had a very long crest on the rear of its head, which was hollow. Air came up the windpipe, looped back along the lower nasal passage to the rear of the crest, forward along the upper nasal passage, and out through the nostril. By adjusting the airflow, the dinosaur may have made its whole head vibrate.

BLOWING ITS OWN TRUMPET
Fossil skulls of *Edmontosaurus* have deep grooves on either side of the nasal area. In life these may have housed loose pouches of skin that could be inflated to balloon out and amplify the vibrations. Some present-day frogs and seals have similar vocal sac resonating systems.

Fossils show the 42.6-foot (13-meter)-long dinosaur probably had good hearing

Nasal bones of skull

Inflatable balloon of skin

Nostril

Edmontosaurus probably made a loud, calling sound like a trumpet

Air blowing up trachea

Plate-shaped head crest

Hole through to right nasal passage

Left nasal passage

PLATE HEAD
Inside the tall, thin crest of *Corythosaurus*, air flowed in a semicircular pattern. The dinosaur would blow just hard enough to set the air in its nasal passages vibrating, and the skull bones with it. This resonance produced and amplified the sounds. The larger the crest, the lower the voice.

Corythosaurus probably made a full, well-rounded sound like a horn

Site of brain inside skull bone

Nostril

BIG EYES
Corythosaurus had large eyes, probably to see the colorful crests of mates and rivals.

LOOK OUT!
Corythosaurus may have used its distinctive call to warn others in its herd of danger.

Airflow up trachea

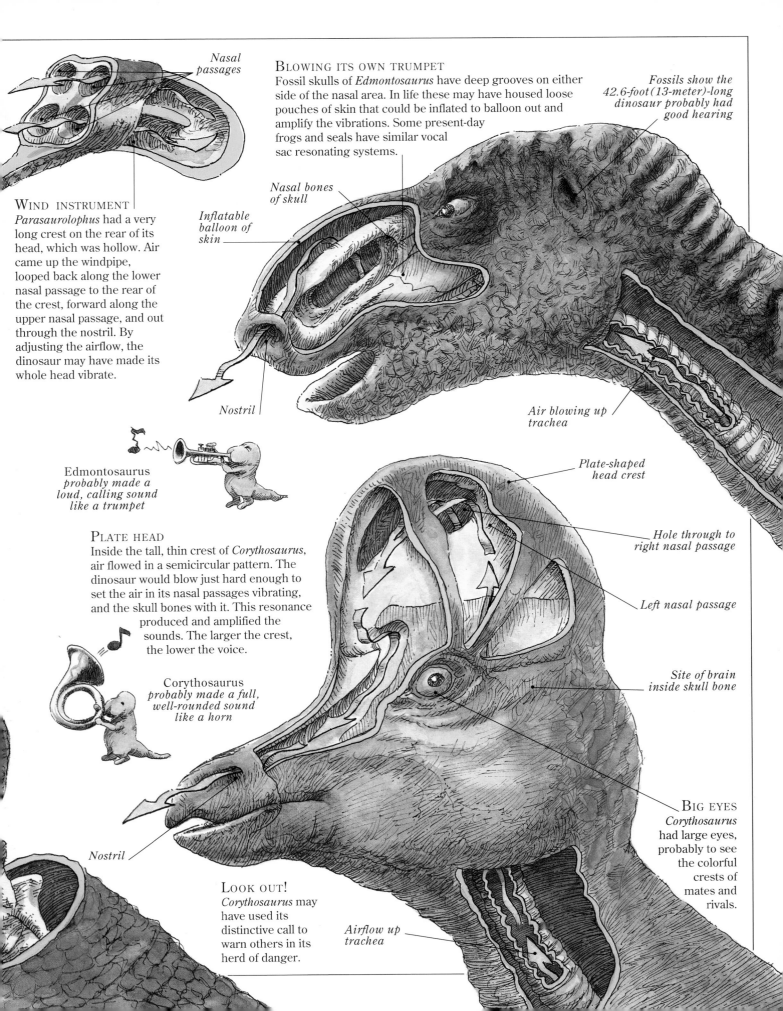

BRAINS AND BODIES

DINOSAURS WERE PROBABLY NOT what we would call clever or intelligent. Overall, these ancient reptiles had big bodies and small brains, not unlike modern-day crocodiles and lizards. But this does not imply failure. In fact, some may have been alert, fast-reacting, and programmed with a nerve system library of instincts and reflexes that enabled them to survive for so long. *Stegosaurus* had a very small brain indeed, yet its kind spread over a wide area and survived for millions of years.

BRIGHT SPARK...
Stenonychosaurus had a relatively large brain in a smallish body. This meant it probably had good control over body movements, fine coordination skills, sharp senses, and even capacity left over for a simple memory bank.

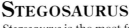

...DIM BULB?
Stegosaurus, on the other hand, was probably not capable of skilled and agile movements. Limited brainpower coupled with sheer bulk would have led to slow reactions, with much of the body "running on automatic."

SMALL AND SPRIGHTLY
Stenonychosaurus was 6.5 feet (2 meters) long and had fast reflexes, which it would have used for hunting lizards and small mammals. The dinosaur's large eyes may indicate that it hunted mainly at dusk or even in the dark.

Powerful hip and leg muscles

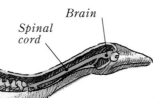

Sharp-clawed grasping hands

Brain

Spinal cord

STEGOSAURUS
Stegosaurus is the most famous small-brain dinosaur. This armored mound of flesh and bone, weighing in at 1.18 tons (1.5 tonnes), and measuring more than 23 feet (7 meters) long, was controlled by a lump of nerves the size of a hen's egg.

HOT PLATE, COLD PLATE
The double row of leaflike plates along the back may have been used for defense, or as part of this dinosaur's body temperature control system (see p. 35).

Scapula (shoulder bone)

Neck vertebrae

Rib

Nerves branching from spinal cord

Spinal cord

Brain

BRAINPOWER
Stegosaurus's body weighed twenty thousand times more than its brain. *Stenonychosaurus*'s body was five hundred times heavier than its brain. Your body is only fifty times heavier than your brain, indicating that your nervous system is highly efficient by comparison.

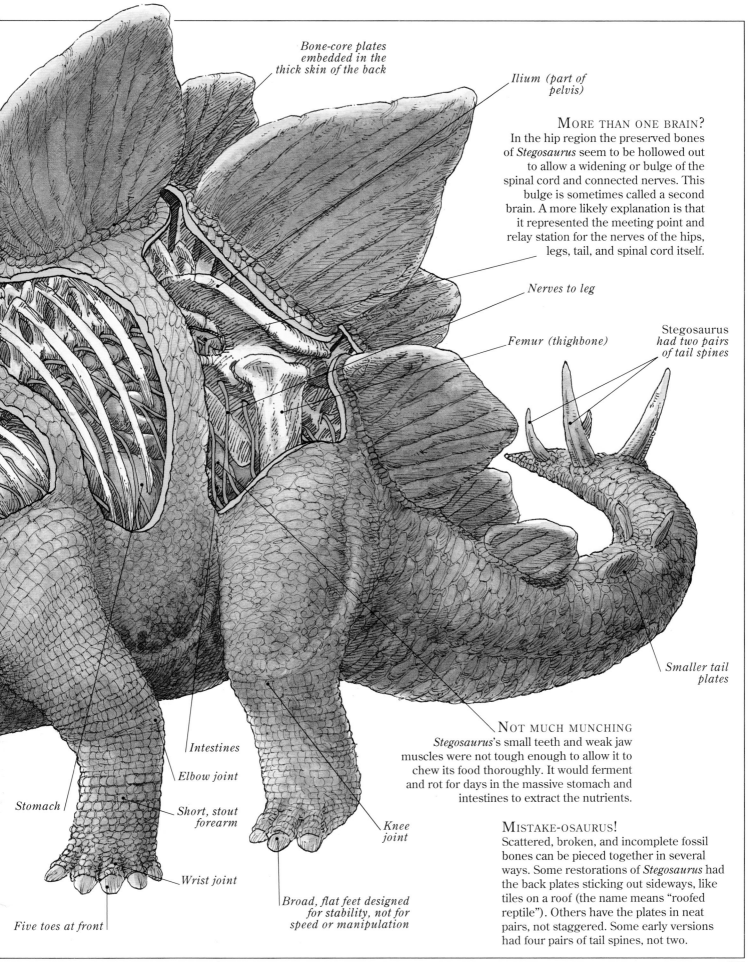

Bone-core plates
embedded in the
thick skin of the back

Ilium (part of
pelvis)

MORE THAN ONE BRAIN?
In the hip region the preserved bones
of *Stegosaurus* seem to be hollowed out
to allow a widening or bulge of the
spinal cord and connected nerves. This
bulge is sometimes called a second
brain. A more likely explanation is that
it represented the meeting point and
relay station for the nerves of the hips,
legs, tail, and spinal cord itself.

Nerves to leg

Femur (thighbone)

Stegosaurus
had two pairs
of tail spines

Smaller tail
plates

NOT MUCH MUNCHING
Stegosaurus's small teeth and weak jaw
muscles were not tough enough to allow it to
chew its food thoroughly. It would ferment
and rot for days in the massive stomach and
intestines to extract the nutrients.

MISTAKE-OSAURUS!
Scattered, broken, and incomplete fossil
bones can be pieced together in several
ways. Some restorations of *Stegosaurus* had
the back plates sticking out sideways, like
tiles on a roof (the name means "roofed
reptile"). Others have the plates in neat
pairs, not staggered. Some early versions
had four pairs of tail spines, not two.

Intestines

Elbow joint

Stomach

Short, stout
forearm

Knee
joint

Wrist joint

Broad, flat feet designed
for stability, not for
speed or manipulation

Five toes at front

SENSITIVE DINOSAURS

AFTER THE SQUISHY DINOSAUR BRAIN rots away, a fossil called an endocast can form to fill the hollows in the skull. This is not quite a brain cast, since a living brain is surrounded by protective tissue and fluid. But there is sufficient similarity to show that dinosaurs had a general brain organization very like that of today's reptiles. Dinosaur endocasts also reveal chambers for the sense organs such as eyes, ears, and especially the nose, as seen in *Camarasaurus*. Far from being stupid, dinosaurs used sharp senses to help them survive.

CAMARASAURUS

A sauropod relation of *Brachiosaurus* and *Diplodocus*, *Camarasaurus* was an inhabitant of western North America about 140 million years ago. It was as tall as five people standing on each other's heads, as long as twelve people lying end to end, and as heavy as 500 people just sitting there.

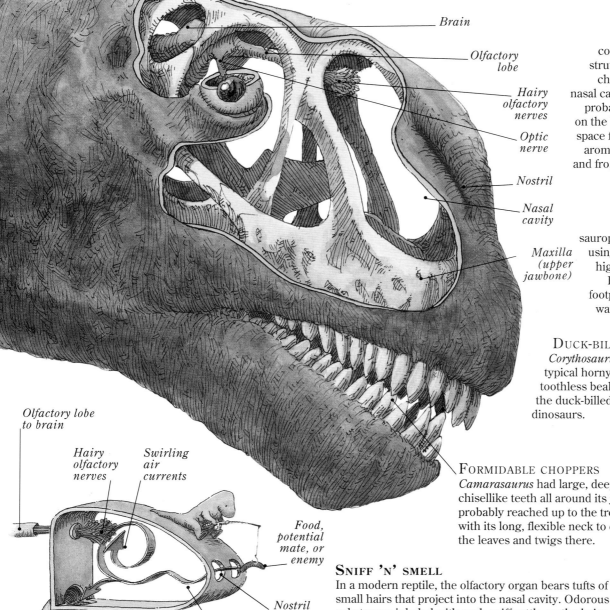

Brain

Olfactory lobe

Hairy olfactory nerves

Optic nerve

Nostril

Nasal cavity

Maxilla (upper jawbone)

BIG NOSE
Camarasaurus's skull consisted mainly of bony struts forming a large, airy chamber at the front, the nasal cavity. The nostrils were probably large and set high on the head. This gave ample space for copious amounts of aroma-bearing air to waft to and fro, on the way in and out of the lungs.

A WASHED-UP IDEA
Experts once thought sauropods lived underwater, using their long necks and high nostrils as snorkels. But fossils of sauropod footprints made in shallow water indicate otherwise.

DUCK-BILL DINO
Corythosaurus had the typical horny, toothless beak of the duck-billed dinosaurs.

Nostril

Olfactory lobe to brain

Hairy olfactory nerves

Swirling air currents

Food, potential mate, or enemy

Nostril

Trachea (windpipe to lungs)

Nasal cavity

FORMIDABLE CHOPPERS
Camarasaurus had large, deep-rooted, chisellike teeth all around its jaws. It probably reached up to the treetops with its long, flexible neck to chop off the leaves and twigs there.

SNIFF 'N' SMELL
In a modern reptile, the olfactory organ bears tufts of small hairs that project into the nasal cavity. Odorous substances inhaled with each sniff settle on the hairs and stimulate nerve signals. These are relayed to the olfactory center of the brain, where smells are identified.

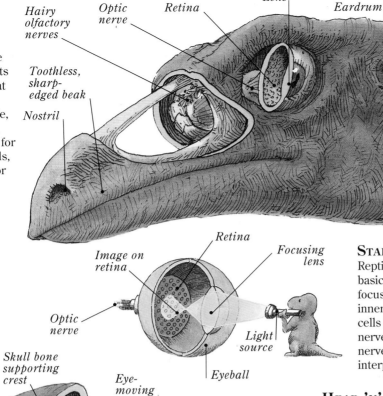

BIG EYES

The eye sockets of *Struthiomimus*, the "ostrich mimic," were proportionally huge. Its endocast indicates that its brain was big, too. This points to a nimble, quick-reacting animal that relied on its eyes for hunting insects, lizards, and other prey, and for spotting enemies.

BENDING BEAK

Struthiomimus's skull bones were light and thin, enabling its birdlike, toothless beak to move with great flexibility.

Hairy olfactory nerves

Optic nerve

Retina

Lens

Eardrum

Toothless, sharp-edged beak

Nostril

BEHIND YOU
Struthiomimus had an extra flexible neck, to turn its head around and see behind.

Image on retina

Retina

Focusing lens

Optic nerve

Light source

Eyeball

STARE 'N' SEE

Reptile eyes are similar in basic design to our own. The lens focuses light rays onto the eyeball's inner lining, the retina. Light-sensitive cells in the retina turn the pattern of rays into nerve signals and send them along the optic nerve to the brain's optic lobes, for interpretation.

HEAR 'N' THERE

Airborne sound waves hit the eardrum or tympanic membrane, making it vibrate. This moves the piston-like stapes bone, which sets up vibrations in the fluid-filled inner ear. Delicate cells in the fluid transform the vibrations into nerve signals that pass along the auditory nerve to the brain's hearing center.

Plate-shaped head crest (featured on p. 25)

Skull bone supporting crest

Eye-moving muscles

Braincase

Eyeball in orbit (socket)

Right inner ear

Right stapes

Right eardrum

Left eardrum

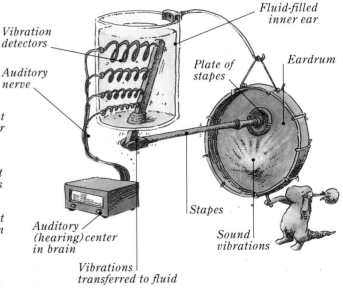

Vibration detectors

Auditory nerve

Fluid-filled inner ear

Plate of stapes

Eardrum

Stapes

Auditory (hearing) center in brain

Vibrations transferred to fluid

Sound vibrations

BIG EARS

If *Corythosaurus* could call to its herd (see p. 25), it must have been able to hear a response. The supporting evidence includes fossil finds of the small, rod-shaped stapes, and a pit or depression in the skull bone that was almost certainly occupied by the ear drum. Remnants of the stapes, and even the shape of the inner ear, have been found in several types of dinosaur.

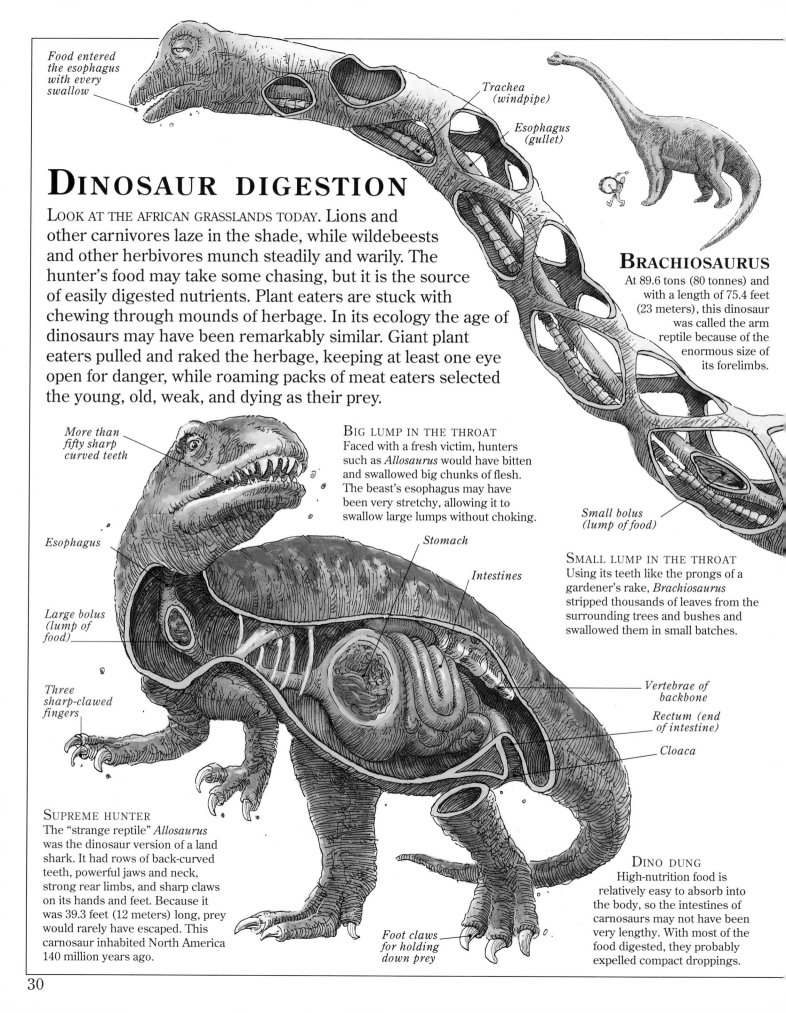

Food entered
the esophagus
with every
swallow

Trachea
(windpipe)

Esophagus
(gullet)

DINOSAUR DIGESTION

LOOK AT THE AFRICAN GRASSLANDS TODAY. Lions and
other carnivores laze in the shade, while wildebeests
and other herbivores munch steadily and warily. The
hunter's food may take some chasing, but it is the source
of easily digested nutrients. Plant eaters are stuck with
chewing through mounds of herbage. In its ecology the age of
dinosaurs may have been remarkably similar. Giant plant
eaters pulled and raked the herbage, keeping at least one eye
open for danger, while roaming packs of meat eaters selected
the young, old, weak, and dying as their prey.

BRACHIOSAURUS
At 89.6 tons (80 tonnes) and
with a length of 75.4 feet
(23 meters), this dinosaur
was called the arm
reptile because of the
enormous size of
its forelimbs.

More than
fifty sharp
curved teeth

BIG LUMP IN THE THROAT
Faced with a fresh victim, hunters
such as *Allosaurus* would have bitten
and swallowed big chunks of flesh.
The beast's esophagus may have
been very stretchy, allowing it to
swallow large lumps without choking.

Small bolus
(lump of food)

Esophagus

Stomach

Intestines

Large bolus
(lump of
food)

SMALL LUMP IN THE THROAT
Using its teeth like the prongs of a
gardener's rake, *Brachiosaurus*
stripped thousands of leaves from the
surrounding trees and bushes and
swallowed them in small batches.

Three
sharp-clawed
fingers

Vertebrae of
backbone

Rectum (end
of intestine)

Cloaca

SUPREME HUNTER
The "strange reptile" *Allosaurus*
was the dinosaur version of a land
shark. It had rows of back-curved
teeth, powerful jaws and neck,
strong rear limbs, and sharp claws
on its hands and feet. Because it
was 39.3 feet (12 meters) long, prey
would rarely have escaped. This
carnosaur inhabited North America
140 million years ago.

Foot claws
for holding
down prey

DINO DUNG
High-nutrition food is
relatively easy to absorb into
the body, so the intestines of
carnosaurs may not have been
very lengthy. With most of the
food digested, they probably
expelled compact droppings.

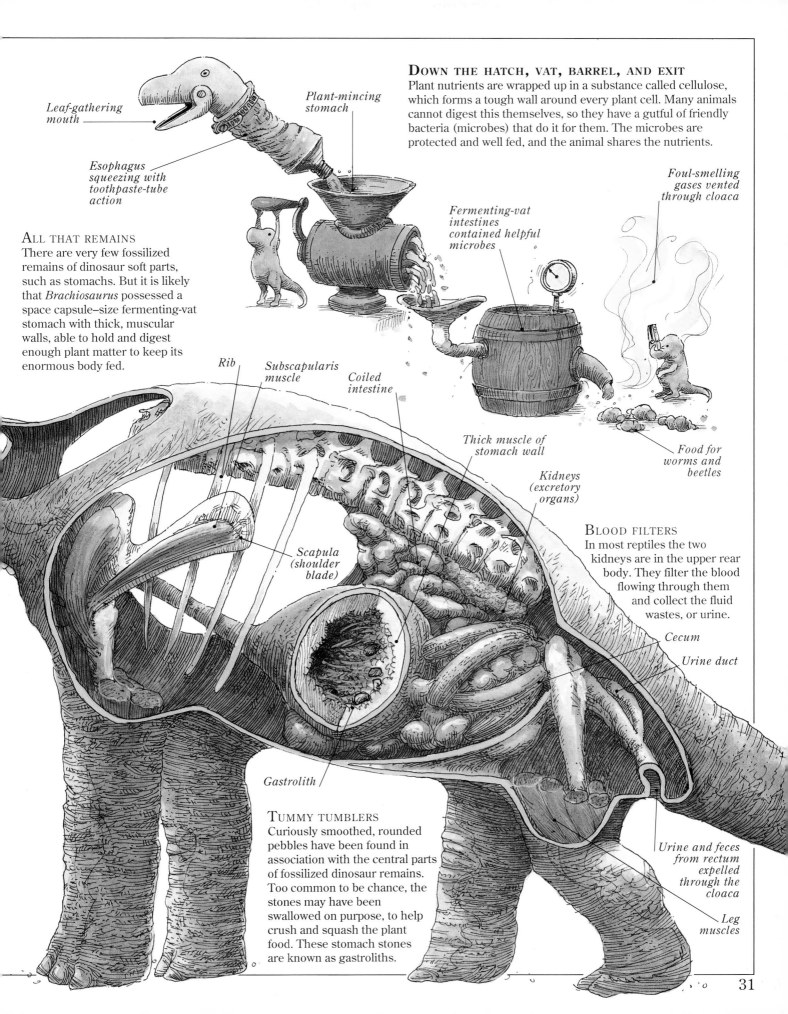

Leaf-gathering mouth

Esophagus squeezing with toothpaste-tube action

Plant-mincing stomach

DOWN THE HATCH, VAT, BARREL, AND EXIT
Plant nutrients are wrapped up in a substance called cellulose, which forms a tough wall around every plant cell. Many animals cannot digest this themselves, so they have a gutful of friendly bacteria (microbes) that do it for them. The microbes are protected and well fed, and the animal shares the nutrients.

Foul-smelling gases vented through cloaca

Fermenting-vat intestines contained helpful microbes

ALL THAT REMAINS
There are very few fossilized remains of dinosaur soft parts, such as stomachs. But it is likely that *Brachiosaurus* possessed a space capsule–size fermenting-vat stomach with thick, muscular walls, able to hold and digest enough plant matter to keep its enormous body fed.

Rib

Subscapularis muscle

Coiled intestine

Thick muscle of stomach wall

Food for worms and beetles

Kidneys (excretory organs)

Scapula (shoulder blade)

BLOOD FILTERS
In most reptiles the two kidneys are in the upper rear body. They filter the blood flowing through them and collect the fluid wastes, or urine.

Cecum

Urine duct

Gastrolith

TUMMY TUMBLERS
Curiously smoothed, rounded pebbles have been found in association with the central parts of fossilized dinosaur remains. Too common to be chance, the stones may have been swallowed on purpose, to help crush and squash the plant food. These stomach stones are known as gastroliths.

Urine and feces from rectum expelled through the cloaca

Leg muscles

BREATHING AND BLOOD

A DINOSAUR'S OXYGEN SUPPLY probably came from breathed-in air. Two lungs absorbed the oxygen, which was then distributed around the body by the heart, blood vessels, and blood. Pushing blood around a body bigger than a truck was hard work for the heart of *Apatosaurus*. Its heart could not have worked like the partly divided heart of some of its reptile relatives; otherwise the same immense pressure needed to push blood up to its brain would have forced blood into its delicate lungs and blown them apart. The heart must have been fully divided into two separate pumps, one powering a high-pressure circuit to the body, the other a low-pressure circuit to the lungs.

APATOSAURUS
This massive beast was 68.8 feet (21 meters) nose to tail, was 16.4 feet (5 meters) high at its hips, and weighed 33.6 tons (30 tonnes). Some of its fossils were once named *Brontosaurus*, but all specimens are now called *Apatosaurus*, or "deceptive reptile"—a good name for a dinosaur that confused the experts.

CAUDAL ARTERY
This huge blood vessel, probably wider than your entire leg, conveyed blood down to the muscles and bones in the dinosaur's tail.

Lung

Pulmonary vein *from lung*

Pulmonary artery to lung

Low-oxygen blood from heart

Pump for low-pressure circuit to lungs

Main veins returned blood to heart

Pump for high-pressure circuit to body

Heart divided into two pumps

Main arteries circulated blood around body

High-oxygen blood to heart

AIR TO BLOOD TO BODY
The dinosaur's lungs expanded like bellows and sucked fresh air in. The low-pressure side of the heart pumped stale, bluish purple blood into the lungs to collect dissolved oxygen from the air. Refreshed and now bright red, the blood returned to the high-pressure side of the heart. From here the blood was pumped around the dinosaur.

Caudal vein

TO THE TIP OF THE TAIL
The tail of *Apatosaurus* had a long line of spinal bones, surrounded by muscles and covered in skin. A network of blood vessels (all that you can see here) carried oxygen and nourishment to all these structures.

Scaly skin covering tail

BRINGING UP THE REAR
When a dinosaur fought off predators by whipping its tail at them, the blood flow increased to supply the active tail muscles.

Network of blood vessels in tail

ELEPHANTINE FEET
Apatosaurus had short, splayed claws and stood flat-footed, in the manner of today's elephant. This spread its body weight—7.08 tons (7 tonnes) on each foot—over a wider area, to prevent the massive creature from sinking into soft ground.

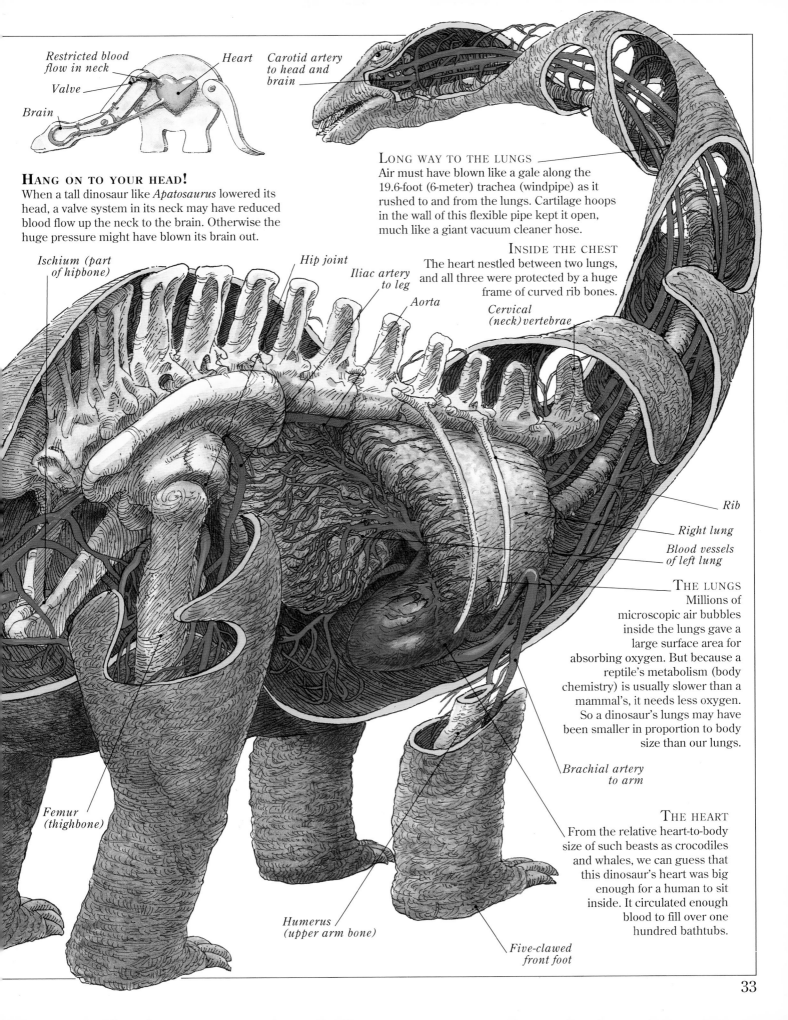

HANG ON TO YOUR HEAD!

When a tall dinosaur like *Apatosaurus* lowered its head, a valve system in its neck may have reduced blood flow up the neck to the brain. Otherwise the huge pressure might have blown its brain out.

Restricted blood flow in neck

Valve

Brain

Heart

Carotid artery to head and brain

LONG WAY TO THE LUNGS
Air must have blown like a gale along the 19.6-foot (6-meter) trachea (windpipe) as it rushed to and from the lungs. Cartilage hoops in the wall of this flexible pipe kept it open, much like a giant vacuum cleaner hose.

INSIDE THE CHEST
The heart nestled between two lungs, and all three were protected by a huge frame of curved rib bones.

Ischium (part of hipbone)

Hip joint

Iliac artery to leg

Aorta

Cervical (neck) vertebrae

Rib

Right lung

Blood vessels of left lung

THE LUNGS
Millions of microscopic air bubbles inside the lungs gave a large surface area for absorbing oxygen. But because a reptile's metabolism (body chemistry) is usually slower than a mammal's, it needs less oxygen. So a dinosaur's lungs may have been smaller in proportion to body size than our lungs.

Brachial artery to arm

THE HEART
From the relative heart-to-body size of such beasts as crocodiles and whales, we can guess that this dinosaur's heart was big enough for a human to sit inside. It circulated enough blood to fill over one hundred bathtubs.

Femur (thighbone)

Humerus (upper arm bone)

Five-clawed front foot

A HEATED DEBATE

MODERN REPTILES ARE COLD-BLOODED. Dinosaurs were reptiles. But were dinosaurs cold-blooded? Probably, but some experts are warming to other ideas. It is likely that most dinosaurs were cold-blooded, or ectothermic, meaning "warmth from without." An ectotherm's body temperature depends on its surroundings. In hot weather it warms up, ready for action. In cold conditions it becomes slow and sluggish. However, many of today's reptiles can regulate their body temperature within certain limits by behavioral methods—basking in the sun or cooling off in the shade. Maybe dinosaurs did the same or, like *Spinosaurus*, kept a secret in their sails.

SPINOSAURUS
This powerfully built, 39.4-foot (12-meter) carnivore dwelled in Africa, some 110 million years ago. Its fossils are not plentiful, but they indicate that it was a carnosaur cousin of the supreme North American hunter *Allosaurus* (see p. 30).

CENTRAL HEATING
As described above, reptiles and many other creatures—from insects to sharks—are ectothermic. Birds and mammals are endothermic, meaning "warmth from within." They generate their own body heat through metabolism. These are the chemical processes that keep an animal's body working.

RAISING THE SAIL
Spinosaurus's huge back sail was supported by flattened bony planks. These are the enlarged dorsal processes projecting from the vertebrae (backbones). Some of these planks are almost 6.6 feet (2 meters) long—as tall as a tall adult!

Dorsal processes grew progressively longer to form sail

Thin skin covering sail allowed quick heat exchange

Iliac part of hipbone

Iliocaudal muscle

Dorsal process of caudal vertebra (tailbone)

Transverse process of caudal vertebra

Blood circulated just under the surface of the sail

Body heat lost through sail

Warmed blood traveled to cold body

WARMING UP
Spinosaurus's extravagant sail may have helped regulate its body temperature by acting as a heat exchanger. To warm itself rapidly, the beast stood sideways to the sun, and its sail soaked up the rays like a solar panel.

COOLING DOWN
If its body became too warm, *Spinosaurus* could stand in the open, breezy shade. The sail worked as a radiator. Blood drew heat from the body, flowed through the sail, and radiated the warmth to the passing air.

RISE AND SHINE
Spinosaurus's temperature control mechanism may have given it an edge over competitors, allowing it to get up and go in the early-morning sun before other cold-blooded creatures—including its prey—shook off the cool of the night.

STEP ON IT
Spinosaurus had strong, pillarlike back legs. The huge claws on its feet may have been used to hold down its struggling prey while the dinosaur's mouth tore off chunks of flesh.

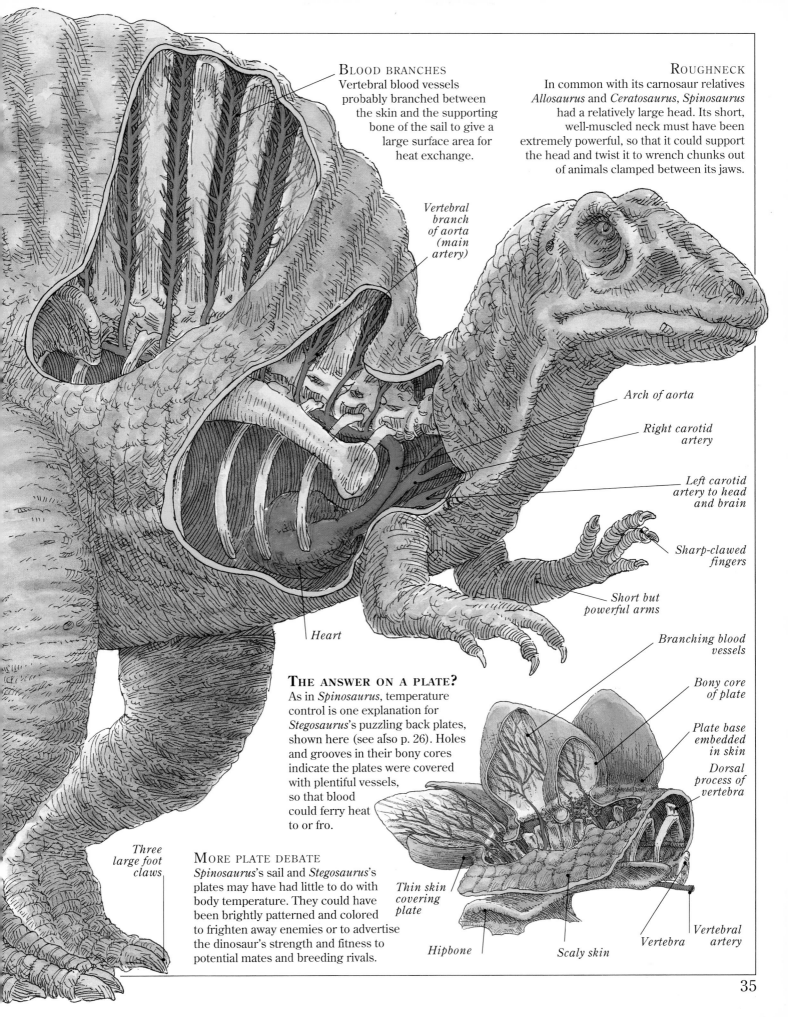

BLOOD BRANCHES
Vertebral blood vessels probably branched between the skin and the supporting bone of the sail to give a large surface area for heat exchange.

ROUGHNECK
In common with its carnosaur relatives *Allosaurus* and *Ceratosaurus*, *Spinosaurus* had a relatively large head. Its short, well-muscled neck must have been extremely powerful, so that it could support the head and twist it to wrench chunks out of animals clamped between its jaws.

Vertebral branch of aorta (main artery)

Arch of aorta

Right carotid artery

Left carotid artery to head and brain

Sharp-clawed fingers

Short but powerful arms

Heart

Branching blood vessels

Bony core of plate

Plate base embedded in skin

Dorsal process of vertebra

THE ANSWER ON A PLATE?
As in *Spinosaurus*, temperature control is one explanation for *Stegosaurus*'s puzzling back plates, shown here (see also p. 26). Holes and grooves in their bony cores indicate the plates were covered with plentiful vessels, so that blood could ferry heat to or fro.

Three large foot claws

MORE PLATE DEBATE
Spinosaurus's sail and *Stegosaurus*'s plates may have had little to do with body temperature. They could have been brightly patterned and colored to frighten away enemies or to advertise the dinosaur's strength and fitness to potential mates and breeding rivals.

Thin skin covering plate

Hipbone

Scaly skin

Vertebra

Vertebral artery

EGGS AND BABIES

DID DINOSAURS LAY EGGS, as their living reptile relatives do? Firm fossil evidence was unearthed in the 1920s in Mongolia's Gobi Desert. Here numerous stony skeletons of the small horned dinosaur *Protoceratops*, ranging from newborn babies to full-grown adults, were found in the sandstone layers—along with nests of perfectly fossilized eggs. These batches of rough-textured, oval eggs were laid carefully in scooped-out hollows in the sand eighty million years ago. Since then eggs of several dinosaur species have been discovered.

FIRST FRILLS
Protoceratops ("first horned face") was a forerunner of the ceratopsian, or horned dinosaur, group, which includes *Triceratops* with its huge neck frill. *Protoceratops*'s frill was already quite large, but the facial horns that give the group its name were only just beginning to evolve, perhaps as a bump on the nose and ridges over the eyes.

Large neck frill

External ear

Nostril

Eyebrow ridge

SNACK SNIPPERS
Protoceratops was probably a herbivoire. The front of its mouth was tipped with a sharp, beak-shaped horn, for snipping up leaves and stems. Powerful jaw muscles worked scissorlike tooth batteries that cut tough plants into pieces. These were swallowed whole, since the teeth were of no use for chewing.

Horny beak

Cheek teeth

Tongue

Yolk sac stored food

Chorion just under shell surrounded rest of egg

Chalky eggshell reduced water loss

Body wastes stored in allantois

Developing baby reptile

Amniotic fluid cushioned and cleaned embryo

Albumen was extra food supply

Amnion

Food supply

Carbon dioxide waste seeped out of egg through shell, membranes, and fluids

Oxygen seeped into egg through shell, membranes, and fluids

Outer capsule

Container for body wastes

Protective cushioning

INSIDE THE EGG(S)
Amphibians lay their soft, jelly-covered eggs in water; they could not survive elsewhere. A reptile egg, with its protective shell, was a great step forward to life on land. The developing baby fed on its yummy yolk in a private pool surrounded by three membranes—from inside out, the amnion, allantois, and chorion. Can you spot the parallels between the real egg and the fully fitted reptile nursery?

FOUR-FOOTED GAIT
Protoceratops almost certainly moved on all fours, supporting its massive weight on its short front and longer rear limbs.

Five-toed front foot

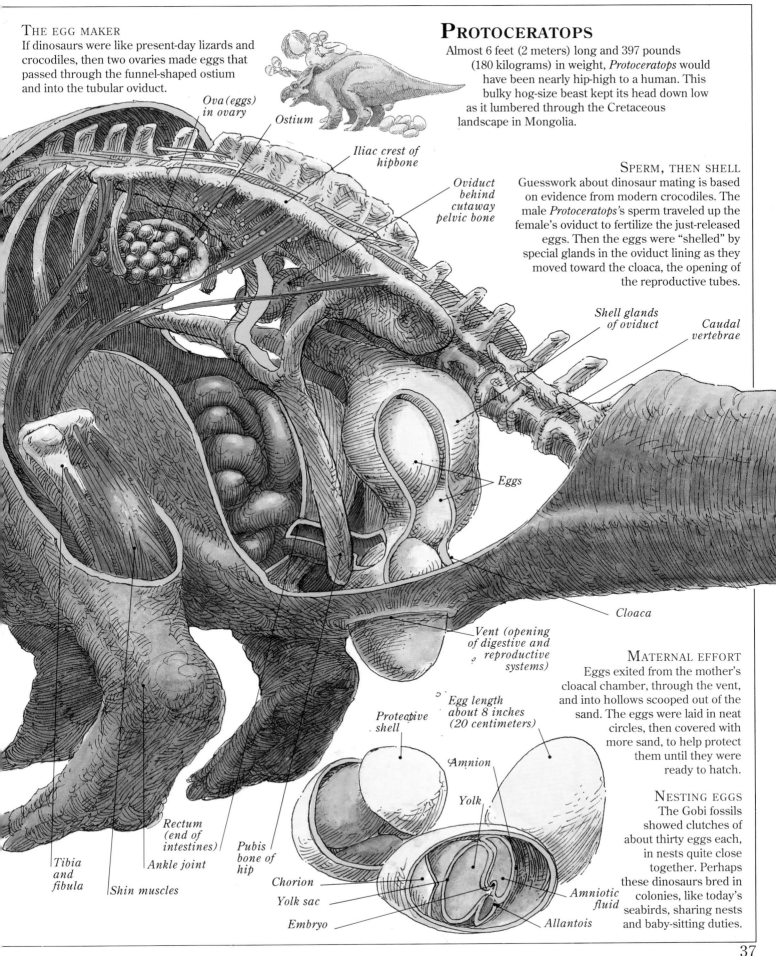

THE EGG MAKER
If dinosaurs were like present-day lizards and crocodiles, then two ovaries made eggs that passed through the funnel-shaped ostium and into the tubular oviduct.

Ova (eggs) in ovary

Ostium

Iliac crest of hipbone

Oviduct behind cutaway pelvic bone

PROTOCERATOPS
Almost 6 feet (2 meters) long and 397 pounds (180 kilograms) in weight, *Protoceratops* would have been nearly hip-high to a human. This bulky hog-size beast kept its head down low as it lumbered through the Cretaceous landscape in Mongolia.

SPERM, THEN SHELL
Guesswork about dinosaur mating is based on evidence from modern crocodiles. The male *Protoceratops*'s sperm traveled up the female's oviduct to fertilize the just-released eggs. Then the eggs were "shelled" by special glands in the oviduct lining as they moved toward the cloaca, the opening of the reproductive tubes.

Shell glands of oviduct

Caudal vertebrae

Eggs

Cloaca

Vent (opening of digestive and reproductive systems)

MATERNAL EFFORT
Eggs exited from the mother's cloacal chamber, through the vent, and into hollows scooped out of the sand. The eggs were laid in neat circles, then covered with more sand, to help protect them until they were ready to hatch.

Egg length about 8 inches (20 centimeters)

Protective shell

Amnion

Yolk

NESTING EGGS
The Gobi fossils showed clutches of about thirty eggs each, in nests quite close together. Perhaps these dinosaurs bred in colonies, like today's seabirds, sharing nests and baby-sitting duties.

Tibia and fibula

Shin muscles

Rectum (end of intestines)

Ankle joint

Pubis bone of hip

Chorion

Yolk sac

Embryo

Amniotic fluid

Allantois

PREHISTORIC OCEANS

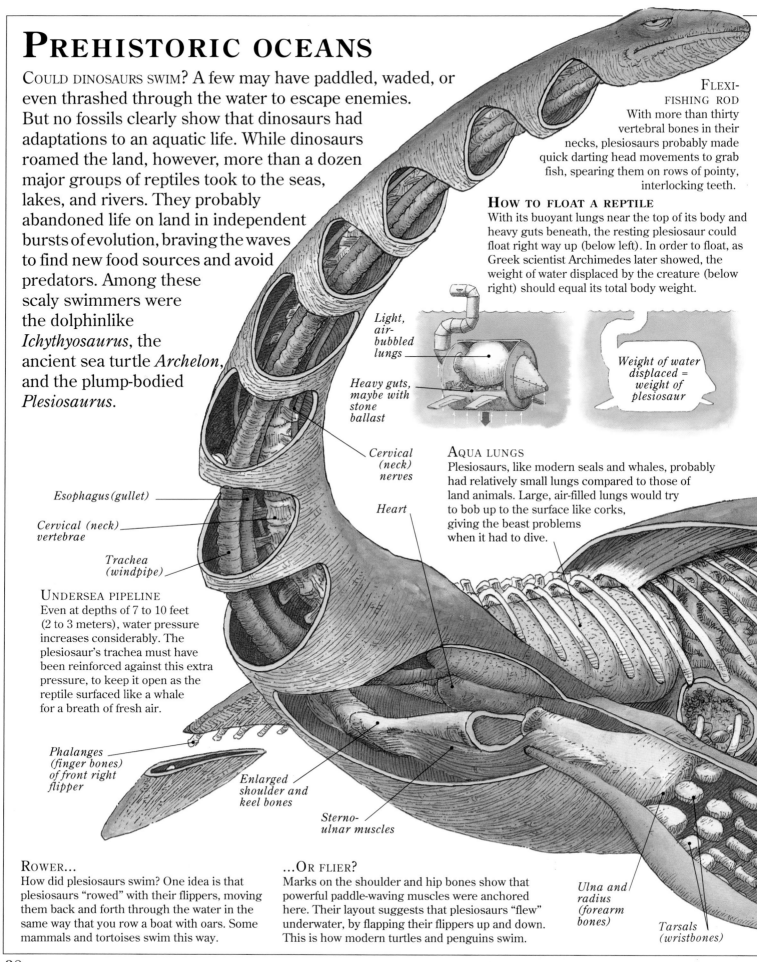

COULD DINOSAURS SWIM? A few may have paddled, waded, or even thrashed through the water to escape enemies. But no fossils clearly show that dinosaurs had adaptations to an aquatic life. While dinosaurs roamed the land, however, more than a dozen major groups of reptiles took to the seas, lakes, and rivers. They probably abandoned life on land in independent bursts of evolution, braving the waves to find new food sources and avoid predators. Among these scaly swimmers were the dolphinlike *Ichythyosaurus*, the ancient sea turtle *Archelon*, and the plump-bodied *Plesiosaurus*.

FLEXI-FISHING ROD
With more than thirty vertebral bones in their necks, plesiosaurs probably made quick darting head movements to grab fish, spearing them on rows of pointy, interlocking teeth.

HOW TO FLOAT A REPTILE
With its buoyant lungs near the top of its body and heavy guts beneath, the resting plesiosaur could float right way up (below left). In order to float, as Greek scientist Archimedes later showed, the weight of water displaced by the creature (below right) should equal its total body weight.

Light, air-bubbled lungs

Heavy guts, maybe with stone ballast

Weight of water displaced = weight of plesiosaur

Cervical (neck) nerves

Heart

Esophagus (gullet)

Cervical (neck) vertebrae

Trachea (windpipe)

AQUA LUNGS
Plesiosaurs, like modern seals and whales, probably had relatively small lungs compared to those of land animals. Large, air-filled lungs would try to bob up to the surface like corks, giving the beast problems when it had to dive.

UNDERSEA PIPELINE
Even at depths of 7 to 10 feet (2 to 3 meters), water pressure increases considerably. The plesiosaur's trachea must have been reinforced against this extra pressure, to keep it open as the reptile surfaced like a whale for a breath of fresh air.

Phalanges (finger bones) of front right flipper

Enlarged shoulder and keel bones

Sterno-ulnar muscles

Ulna and radius (forearm bones)

Tarsals (wristbones)

ROWER...
How did plesiosaurs swim? One idea is that plesiosaurs "rowed" with their flippers, moving them back and forth through the water in the same way that you row a boat with oars. Some mammals and tortoises swim this way.

...OR FLIER?
Marks on the shoulder and hip bones show that powerful paddle-waving muscles were anchored here. Their layout suggests that plesiosaurs "flew" underwater, by flapping their flippers up and down. This is how modern turtles and penguins swim.

THE FISHLIKE SWISH
Ichthyosaurs, the "fish reptiles," probably used their finlike limbs for steering but not for swimming. Propulsive power came from muscles along the sides of the backbones that worked the fishlike tail, swishing it strongly from side to side.

Dorsal fin for stability

WATER BABIES
Unlike other reptiles, which lay eggs on land, a mother ichthyosaur gave birth to live young in the water—tail first, like modern porpoises.

KINKY TAIL
The tailbones (caudal vertebrae) bent down into the lower of the two tail lobes. This may have helped to drive the ichthyosaur head-up in the water with each tail swing. In sharks, the backbone kinks into the upper tail lobe.

Pointed, streamlined snout

Pelvic fin

Intestines

Stomach

Caudal (tail) vertebrae

Pectoral fin

Stiffening fin-ray bones

FISH SUPPERS
Like plesiosaurs and the fish-fancying dinosaur *Baryonyx* (p. 21), ichthyosaurs had rows of slim, sharp teeth to grasp their slippery, wriggling prey.

CONVERGENT EVOLUTION
Sharks, other fast fish, dolphins, and ichthyosaurs have remarkably similar overall shapes, even though they are quite different inside. They are streamlined to slip through the water as speedily as possible. This outer similarity is termed convergent evolution.

PLESIOSAURUS
The first professional fossil hunter, Mary Anning, found not only the earliest known remains of an ichthyosaur, but also uncovered a nearly complete skeleton of the first *Plesiosaurus* ("near reptile") close to her home on the southern coast of England. The plesiosaurs, up to 46 feet (14 meters) long, thrived in the Jurassic and Cretaceous periods.

Ribs

Intestines

Femur

Leg flipper

TAILING OFF
The typical plesiosaur tail was of medium length, tapering, and stiff. It was not used for propulsion, but was simply a smoothly pointed end to the body, to help with streamlining in the high-resistance aquatic environment.

DOUBLE PROTECTION
The protective bony shell is called the carapace on the back, and the plastron on the underside.

Gastralia (stomach ribs)

BELLY BALLAST?
Plesiosaurs may have swallowed seabed pebbles, to give them ballast low in the body as well as to help grind up their food.

Vertebrae and ribs fused to inside of shell

Tiny, useless tail

HANDY FLIPPERS
The flipper bones resemble those in your own hand, though their shapes are broader and flatter to give an oarlike paddle.

Leg flipper

EARLY TURTLE
Archelon, almost 13 feet (4 meters) long, paddled through the Cretaceous seas about 80 million years ago. It had large, flipperlike front limbs, a tough shell, and a curved, horny beak that may have trapped shellfish.

Lung

Arm and hand bones in front flipper

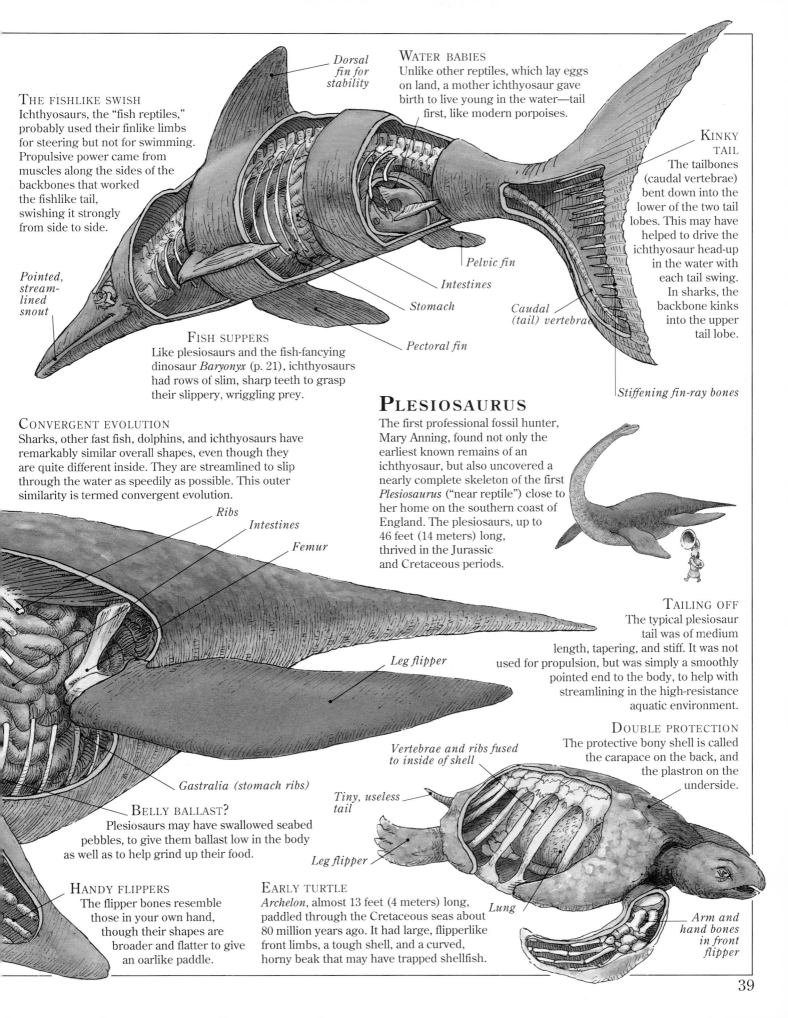

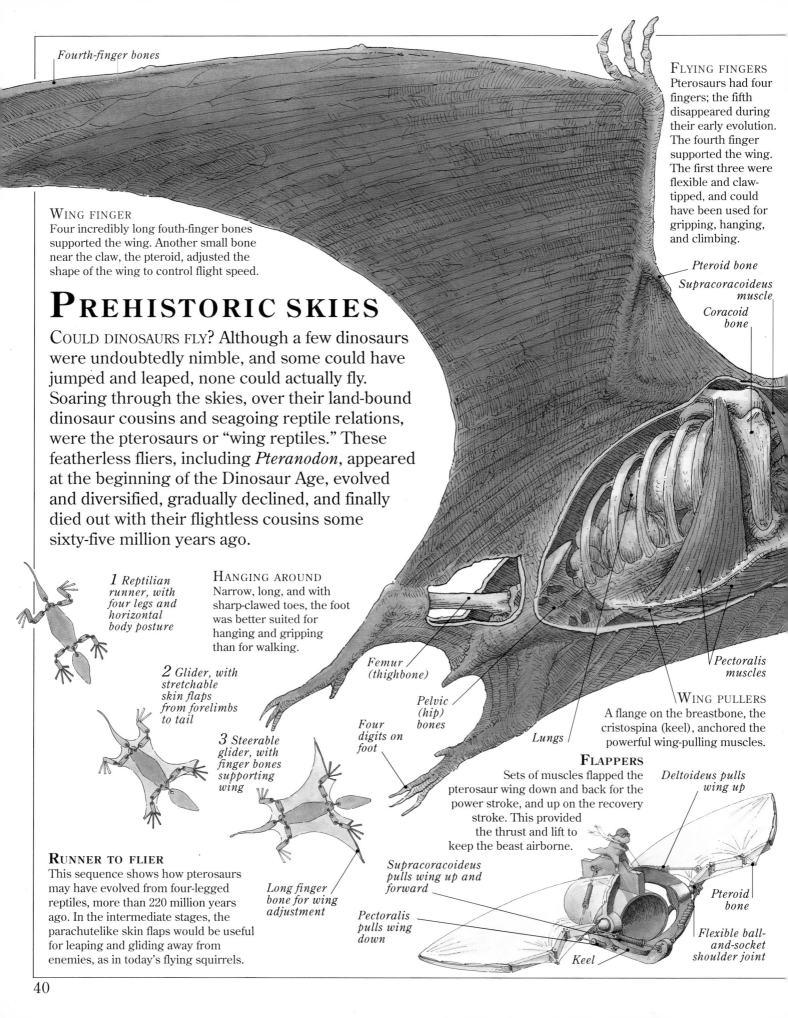

Fourth-finger bones

WING FINGER
Four incredibly long fouth-finger bones supported the wing. Another small bone near the claw, the pteroid, adjusted the shape of the wing to control flight speed.

PREHISTORIC SKIES

COULD DINOSAURS FLY? Although a few dinosaurs were undoubtedly nimble, and some could have jumped and leaped, none could actually fly. Soaring through the skies, over their land-bound dinosaur cousins and seagoing reptile relations, were the pterosaurs or "wing reptiles." These featherless fliers, including *Pteranodon*, appeared at the beginning of the Dinosaur Age, evolved and diversified, gradually declined, and finally died out with their flightless cousins some sixty-five million years ago.

1 Reptilian runner, with four legs and horizontal body posture

HANGING AROUND
Narrow, long, and with sharp-clawed toes, the foot was better suited for hanging and gripping than for walking.

2 Glider, with stretchable skin flaps from forelimbs to tail

3 Steerable glider, with finger bones supporting wing

RUNNER TO FLIER
This sequence shows how pterosaurs may have evolved from four-legged reptiles, more than 220 million years ago. In the intermediate stages, the parachutelike skin flaps would be useful for leaping and gliding away from enemies, as in today's flying squirrels.

Long finger bone for wing adjustment

FLYING FINGERS
Pterosaurs had four fingers; the fifth disappeared during their early evolution. The fourth finger supported the wing. The first three were flexible and claw-tipped, and could have been used for gripping, hanging, and climbing.

Pteroid bone
Supracoracoideus muscle
Coracoid bone

Femur (thighbone)
Pelvic (hip) bones
Four digits on foot
Lungs

Pectoralis muscles

WING PULLERS
A flange on the breastbone, the cristospina (keel), anchored the powerful wing-pulling muscles.

FLAPPERS
Sets of muscles flapped the pterosaur wing down and back for the power stroke, and up on the recovery stroke. This provided the thrust and lift to keep the beast airborne.

Supracoracoideus pulls wing up and forward

Pectoralis pulls wing down

Deltoideus pulls wing up

Pteroid bone

Flexible ball-and-socket shoulder joint

Keel

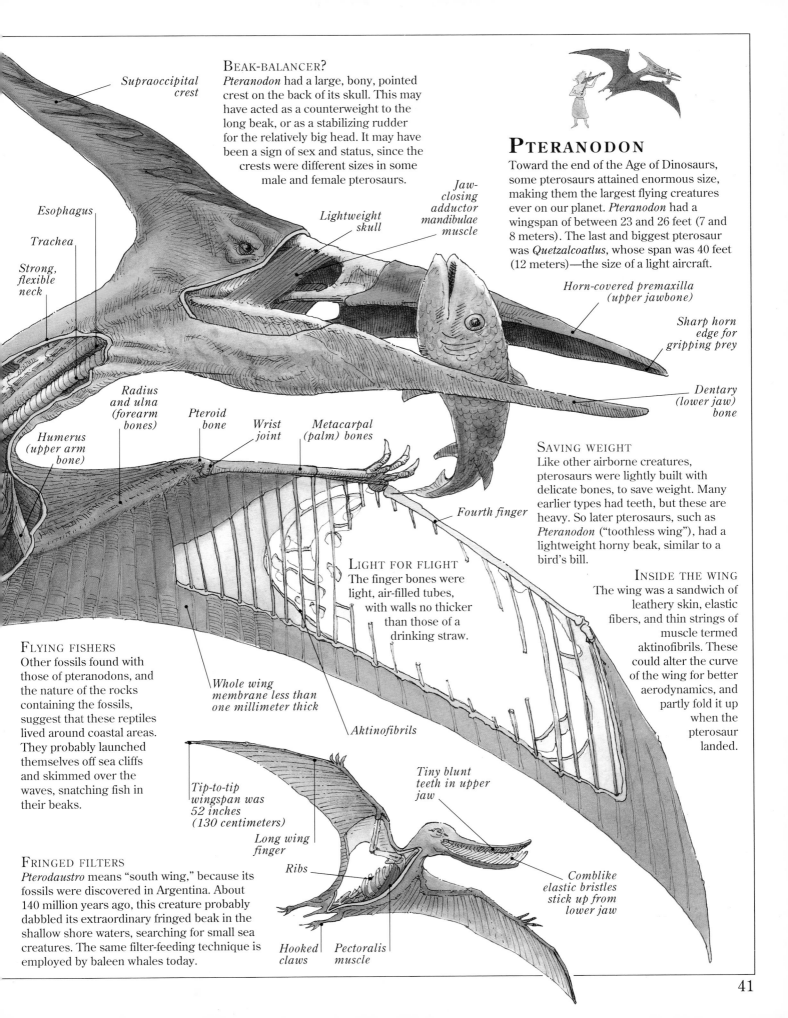

BEAK-BALANCER?
Pteranodon had a large, bony, pointed crest on the back of its skull. This may have acted as a counterweight to the long beak, or as a stabilizing rudder for the relatively big head. It may have been a sign of sex and status, since the crests were different sizes in some male and female pterosaurs.

Supraoccipital crest

Esophagus

Trachea

Strong, flexible neck

Lightweight skull

Jaw-closing adductor mandibulae muscle

Radius and ulna (forearm bones)

Humerus (upper arm bone)

Pteroid bone

Wrist joint

Metacarpal (palm) bones

PTERANODON

Toward the end of the Age of Dinosaurs, some pterosaurs attained enormous size, making them the largest flying creatures ever on our planet. *Pteranodon* had a wingspan of between 23 and 26 feet (7 and 8 meters). The last and biggest pterosaur was *Quetzalcoatlus*, whose span was 40 feet (12 meters)—the size of a light aircraft.

Horn-covered premaxilla (upper jawbone)

Sharp horn edge for gripping prey

Dentary (lower jaw) bone

SAVING WEIGHT
Like other airborne creatures, pterosaurs were lightly built with delicate bones, to save weight. Many earlier types had teeth, but these are heavy. So later pterosaurs, such as *Pteranodon* ("toothless wing"), had a lightweight horny beak, similar to a bird's bill.

Fourth finger

LIGHT FOR FLIGHT
The finger bones were light, air-filled tubes, with walls no thicker than those of a drinking straw.

INSIDE THE WING
The wing was a sandwich of leathery skin, elastic fibers, and thin strings of muscle termed aktinofibrils. These could alter the curve of the wing for better aerodynamics, and partly fold it up when the pterosaur landed.

FLYING FISHERS
Other fossils found with those of pteranodons, and the nature of the rocks containing the fossils, suggest that these reptiles lived around coastal areas. They probably launched themselves off sea cliffs and skimmed over the waves, snatching fish in their beaks.

Whole wing membrane less than one millimeter thick

Aktinofibrils

Tip-to-tip wingspan was 52 inches (130 centimeters)

Long wing finger

Ribs

Tiny blunt teeth in upper jaw

Comblike elastic bristles stick up from lower jaw

FRINGED FILTERS
Pterodaustro means "south wing," because its fossils were discovered in Argentina. About 140 million years ago, this creature probably dabbled its extraordinary fringed beak in the shallow shore waters, searching for small sea creatures. The same filter-feeding technique is employed by baleen whales today.

Hooked claws

Pectoralis muscle

CREEPY-CRAWLIES

WHAT'S OLDER THAN A DINOSAUR? Long before any backboned creatures—whether amphibian or reptile—set foot on land, invertebrates (animals without backbones) crept across the Earth. Among the first were arthropods, animals with a hard outer body casing and jointed legs. They included centipedes, millipedes, mites, ticks, scorpions, and insects. With a 400-million-year history, land arthropods far outlived the dinosaurs, and still survive in incredible numbers. Today these small scurriers are sometimes called "mini-beasts." But some mini-beasts once reached maxi-sizes—this centipede was longer than your leg!

GIANT CENTIPEDE

Centipedes make up the group Chilopoda. They first crawled the land 250 million years ago. Today these creatures grow to about 10 inches (25 centimeters) long, but their ancient cousins reached over 3 feet (one meter) in length.

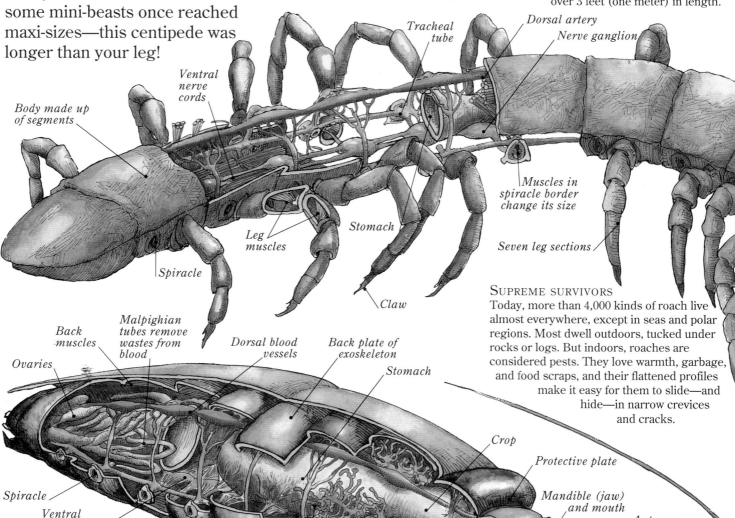

Tracheal tube

Dorsal artery

Nerve ganglion

Ventral nerve cords

Body made up of segments

Muscles in spiracle border change its size

Leg muscles

Stomach

Seven leg sections

Spiracle

Claw

Malpighian tubes remove wastes from blood

Back muscles

Ovaries

Dorsal blood vessels

Back plate of exoskeleton

Stomach

Crop

Protective plate

Spiracle

Ventral nerve cord

Mandible (jaw) and mouth

Antenna

Leg muscles

Leg-flexing thorax muscle

Pharyngeal (sucking) muscles

Maxilla senses and holds food

Pyloric ceca carry nutrients from digested food

Five main foot sections

Gripping claw

SUPREME SURVIVORS
Today, more than 4,000 kinds of roach live almost everywhere, except in seas and polar regions. Most dwell outdoors, tucked under rocks or logs. But indoors, roaches are considered pests. They love warmth, garbage, and food scraps, and their flattened profiles make it easy for them to slide—and hide—in narrow crevices and cracks.

AN EXTENSIVE MENU
Much of the cockroaches' success is due to their versatile mouthparts. The mandibles or jaws are simple but strong chewers, which can deal with a variety of foods, from meat fibers to bread crumbs, leather, paper—even solid wood.

COCKROACH
These "bugs" from the insect group Blattodea have changed little over 300 million years. The biggest roaches were hand-sized, but today none grows longer than 3 inches (8 centimeters).

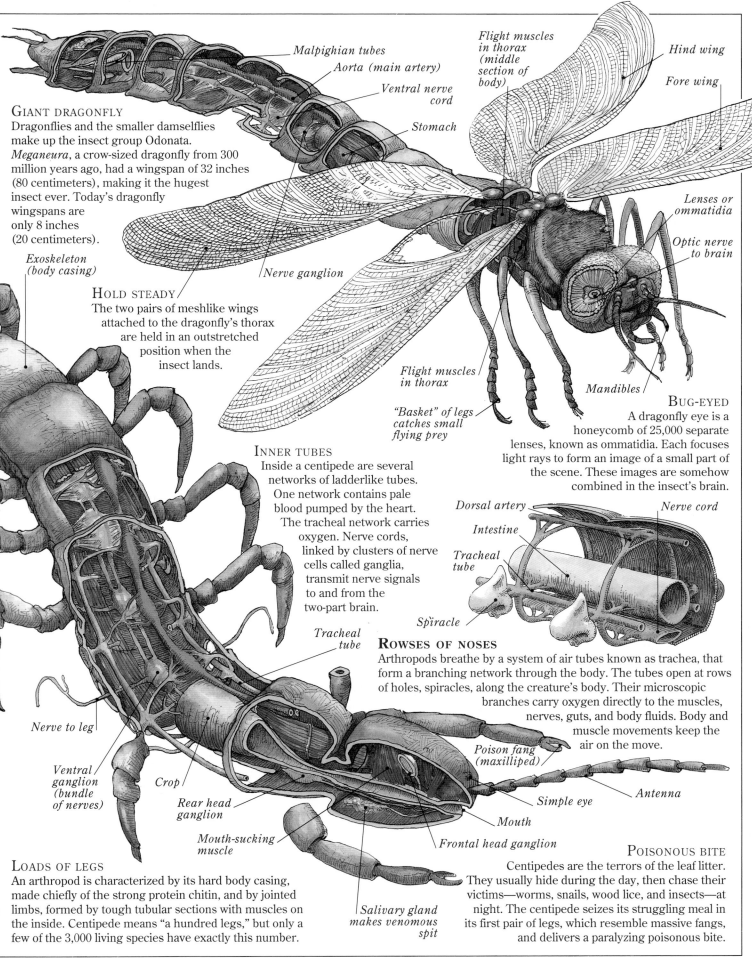

Malpighian tubes

Aorta (main artery)

Ventral nerve cord

Stomach

Flight muscles in thorax (middle section of body)

Hind wing

Fore wing

Lenses or ommatidia

Optic nerve to brain

GIANT DRAGONFLY

Dragonflies and the smaller damselflies make up the insect group Odonata. *Meganeura*, a crow-sized dragonfly from 300 million years ago, had a wingspan of 32 inches (80 centimeters), making it the hugest insect ever. Today's dragonfly wingspans are only 8 inches (20 centimeters).

Exoskeleton (body casing)

Nerve ganglion

HOLD STEADY
The two pairs of meshlike wings attached to the dragonfly's thorax are held in an outstretched position when the insect lands.

Flight muscles in thorax

"Basket" of legs catches small flying prey

Mandibles

BUG-EYED
A dragonfly eye is a honeycomb of 25,000 separate lenses, known as ommatidia. Each focuses light rays to form an image of a small part of the scene. These images are somehow combined in the insect's brain.

INNER TUBES
Inside a centipede are several networks of ladderlike tubes. One network contains pale blood pumped by the heart. The tracheal network carries oxygen. Nerve cords, linked by clusters of nerve cells called ganglia, transmit nerve signals to and from the two-part brain.

Dorsal artery

Intestine

Tracheal tube

Spiracle

Nerve cord

ROWSES OF NOSES
Arthropods breathe by a system of air tubes known as trachea, that form a branching network through the body. The tubes open at rows of holes, spiracles, along the creature's body. Their microscopic branches carry oxygen directly to the muscles, nerves, guts, and body fluids. Body and muscle movements keep the air on the move.

Tracheal tube

Nerve to leg

Ventral ganglion (bundle of nerves)

Crop

Rear head ganglion

Mouth-sucking muscle

Poison fang (maxilliped)

Simple eye

Antenna

Mouth

Frontal head ganglion

Salivary gland makes venomous spit

LOADS OF LEGS
An arthropod is characterized by its hard body casing, made chiefly of the strong protein chitin, and by jointed limbs, formed by tough tubular sections with muscles on the inside. Centipede means "a hundred legs," but only a few of the 3,000 living species have exactly this number.

POISONOUS BITE
Centipedes are the terrors of the leaf litter. They usually hide during the day, then chase their victims—worms, snails, wood lice, and insects—at night. The centipede seizes its struggling meal in its first pair of legs, which resemble massive fangs, and delivers a paralyzing poisonous bite.

43

FUR AND FEATHER

FUR MEANS MAMMAL, and feathers mean bird. But it's not always so clear-cut. Extinct animals must be classified on the basis of their fossil remains. From the details of its teeth, jaw, and ear bones, we know that *Probelesodon* shown here is technically a reptile. Yet its fossils imply that it was so far along the road to becoming a mammal, it had fur and whiskers. The famous flying *Archaeopteryx* also had reptilian features, such as teeth, wing claws, and a chain of tailbones, which modern birds lack. But its fossilized feathers mark it out as the earliest known bird.

ARCHAEOPTERYX

Only six fossil specimens of the chicken-size "ancient wing" have been found, all from southeast Germany. Feathers aside, they are so similar to reptiles that some were first identified as small pterosaurs, or dinosaurs such as *Compsognathus*. The remains are 150 million years old.

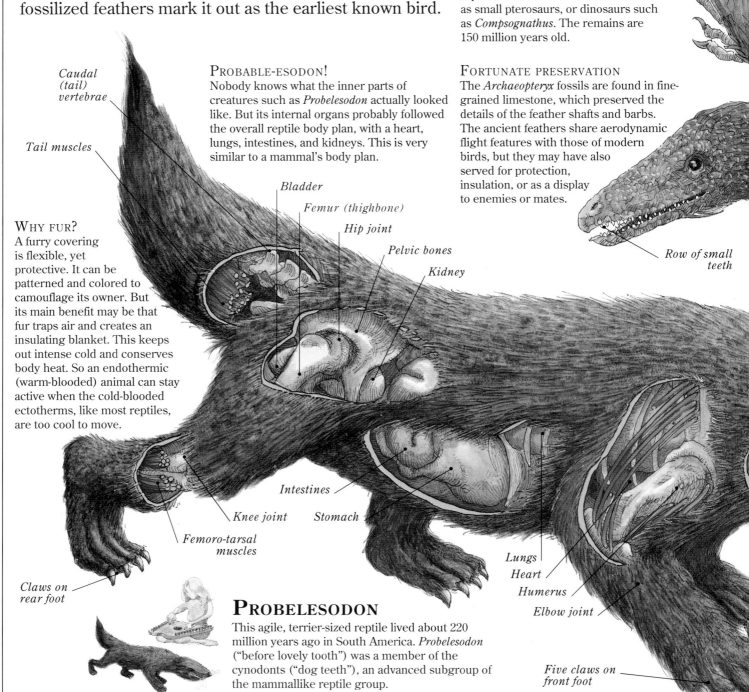

PROBABLE-ESODON!
Nobody knows what the inner parts of creatures such as *Probelesodon* actually looked like. But its internal organs probably followed the overall reptile body plan, with a heart, lungs, intestines, and kidneys. This is very similar to a mammal's body plan.

FORTUNATE PRESERVATION
The *Archaeopteryx* fossils are found in fine-grained limestone, which preserved the details of the feather shafts and barbs. The ancient feathers share aerodynamic flight features with those of modern birds, but they may have also served for protection, insulation, or as a display to enemies or mates.

Caudal (tail) vertebrae

Tail muscles

WHY FUR?
A furry covering is flexible, yet protective. It can be patterned and colored to camouflage its owner. But its main benefit may be that fur traps air and creates an insulating blanket. This keeps out intense cold and conserves body heat. So an endothermic (warm-blooded) animal can stay active when the cold-blooded ectotherms, like most reptiles, are too cool to move.

Bladder

Femur (thighbone)

Hip joint

Pelvic bones

Kidney

Row of small teeth

Intestines

Knee joint   *Stomach*

Femoro-tarsal muscles

Claws on rear foot

Lungs
Heart
Humerus
Elbow joint

PROBELESODON

This agile, terrier-sized reptile lived about 220 million years ago in South America. *Probelesodon* ("before lovely tooth") was a member of the cynodonts ("dog teeth"), an advanced subgroup of the mammallike reptile group.

Five claws on front foot

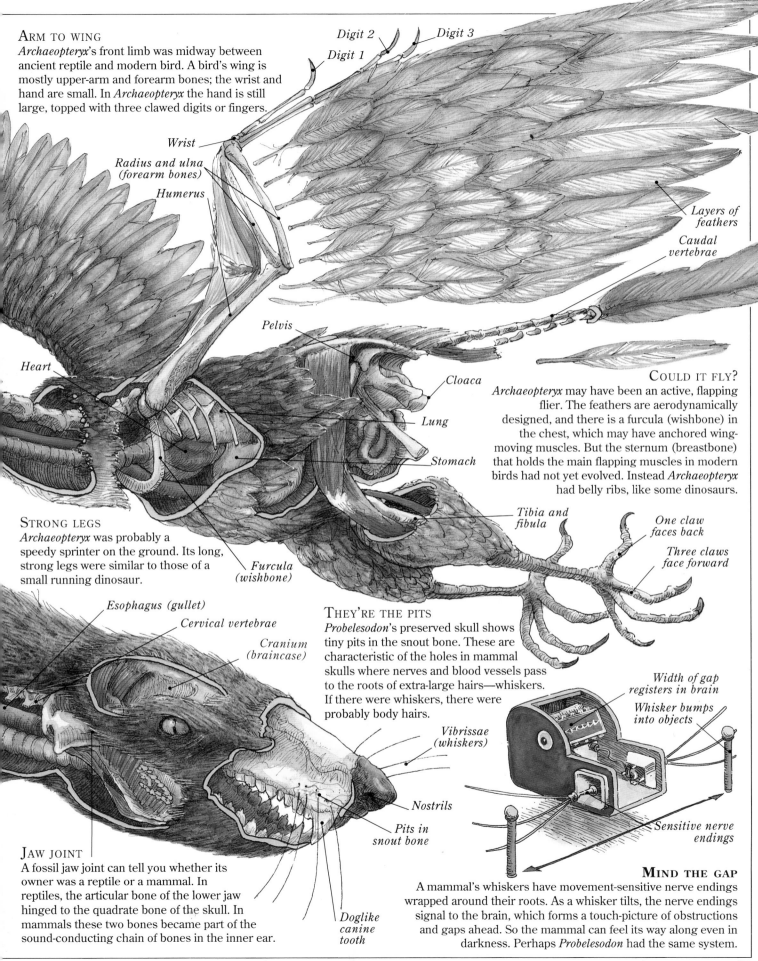

ARM TO WING
Archaeopteryx's front limb was midway between ancient reptile and modern bird. A bird's wing is mostly upper-arm and forearm bones; the wrist and hand are small. In *Archaeopteryx* the hand is still large, topped with three clawed digits or fingers.

Digit 2

Digit 3

Digit 1

Wrist

Radius and ulna (forearm bones)

Humerus

Layers of feathers

Caudal vertebrae

Heart

Pelvis

Cloaca

Lung

Stomach

COULD IT FLY?
Archaeopteryx may have been an active, flapping flier. The feathers are aerodynamically designed, and there is a furcula (wishbone) in the chest, which may have anchored wing-moving muscles. But the sternum (breastbone) that holds the main flapping muscles in modern birds had not yet evolved. Instead *Archaeopteryx* had belly ribs, like some dinosaurs.

Tibia and fibula

One claw faces back

Three claws face forward

STRONG LEGS
Archaeopteryx was probably a speedy sprinter on the ground. Its long, strong legs were similar to those of a small running dinosaur.

Furcula (wishbone)

Esophagus (gullet)

Cervical vertebrae

Cranium (braincase)

THEY'RE THE PITS
Probelesodon's preserved skull shows tiny pits in the snout bone. These are characteristic of the holes in mammal skulls where nerves and blood vessels pass to the roots of extra-large hairs—whiskers. If there were whiskers, there were probably body hairs.

Width of gap registers in brain

Whisker bumps into objects

Vibrissae (whiskers)

Nostrils

Pits in snout bone

Sensitive nerve endings

JAW JOINT
A fossil jaw joint can tell you whether its owner was a reptile or a mammal. In reptiles, the articular bone of the lower jaw hinged to the quadrate bone of the skull. In mammals these two bones became part of the sound-conducting chain of bones in the inner ear.

Doglike canine tooth

MIND THE GAP
A mammal's whiskers have movement-sensitive nerve endings wrapped around their roots. As a whisker tilts, the nerve endings signal to the brain, which forms a touch-picture of obstructions and gaps ahead. So the mammal can feel its way along even in darkness. Perhaps *Probelesodon* had the same system.

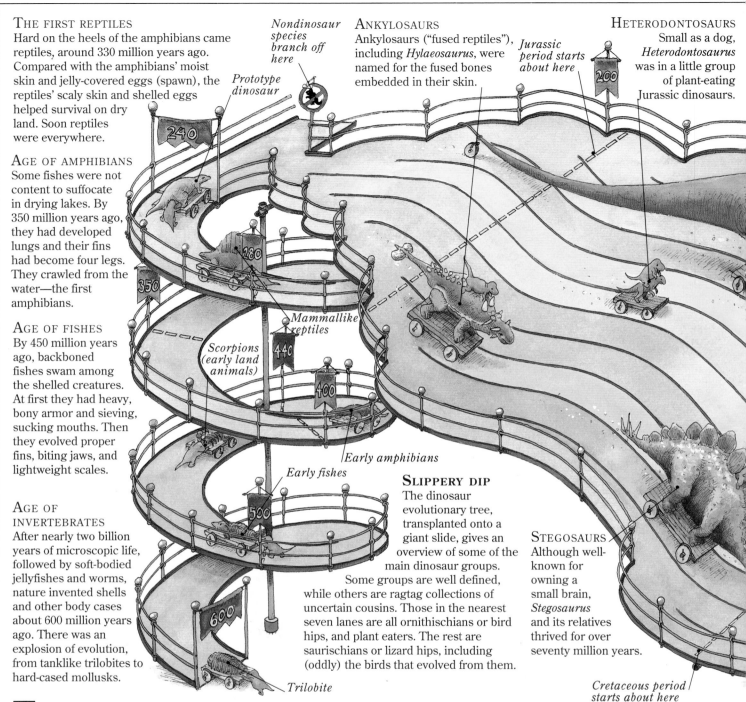

THE FIRST REPTILES
Hard on the heels of the amphibians came reptiles, around 330 million years ago. Compared with the amphibians' moist skin and jelly-covered eggs (spawn), the reptiles' scaly skin and shelled eggs helped survival on dry land. Soon reptiles were everywhere.

AGE OF AMPHIBIANS
Some fishes were not content to suffocate in drying lakes. By 350 million years ago, they had developed lungs and their fins had become four legs. They crawled from the water—the first amphibians.

AGE OF FISHES
By 450 million years ago, backboned fishes swam among the shelled creatures. At first they had heavy, bony armor and sieving, sucking mouths. Then they evolved proper fins, biting jaws, and lightweight scales.

AGE OF INVERTEBRATES
After nearly two billion years of microscopic life, followed by soft-bodied jellyfishes and worms, nature invented shells and other body cases about 600 million years ago. There was an explosion of evolution, from tanklike trilobites to hard-cased mollusks.

Nondinosaur species branch off here

Prototype dinosaur

ANKYLOSAURS
Ankylosaurs ("fused reptiles"), including *Hylaeosaurus*, were named for the fused bones embedded in their skin.

Jurassic period starts about here

HETERODONTOSAURS
Small as a dog, *Heterodontosaurus* was in a little group of plant-eating Jurassic dinosaurs.

Mammallike reptiles

Scorpions (early land animals)

Early amphibians

Early fishes

SLIPPERY DIP
The dinosaur evolutionary tree, transplanted onto a giant slide, gives an overview of some of the main dinosaur groups. Some groups are well defined, while others are ragtag collections of uncertain cousins. Those in the nearest seven lanes are all ornithischians or bird hips, and plant eaters. The rest are saurischians or lizard hips, including (oddly) the birds that evolved from them.

Trilobite

STEGOSAURS
Although well-known for owning a small brain, *Stegosaurus* and its relatives thrived for over seventy million years.

Cretaceous period starts about here

THE SLIDE TO EXTINCTION

LIFE IS A SLIPPERY SLIDE toward death. A cat may live ten years, a giant tortoise one hundred years, and a huge tree 1,000 years. On the vastly longer time scale of Earth history, whole groups of living things evolve, flourish, and die. Humans have been around for scarcely two million years. Dinosaurs outdid us—nearly eighty times longer. More than 1,000 kinds or species of dinosaur came and went during the Mesozoic Era. Despite their numbers, variety, and adaptability, they could not cope with some type of change at the end of the Cretaceous period. Even the ultra-successful dinosaurs succumbed in the end.

THE DINOSAUR AGE
Prehistory is divided into time chunks known as eras, which are split into periods. Dinosaurs lived in the Mesozoic Era, from 64 million to around 240 million years ago. This comprised three periods: the Triassic (198 to 240 million years ago), when dinosaurs first appeared; the Jurassic (135 to 198 million years ago), heyday of the huge plant eaters; and the Cretaceous (64 to 135 million years ago), which closed with their extinction.

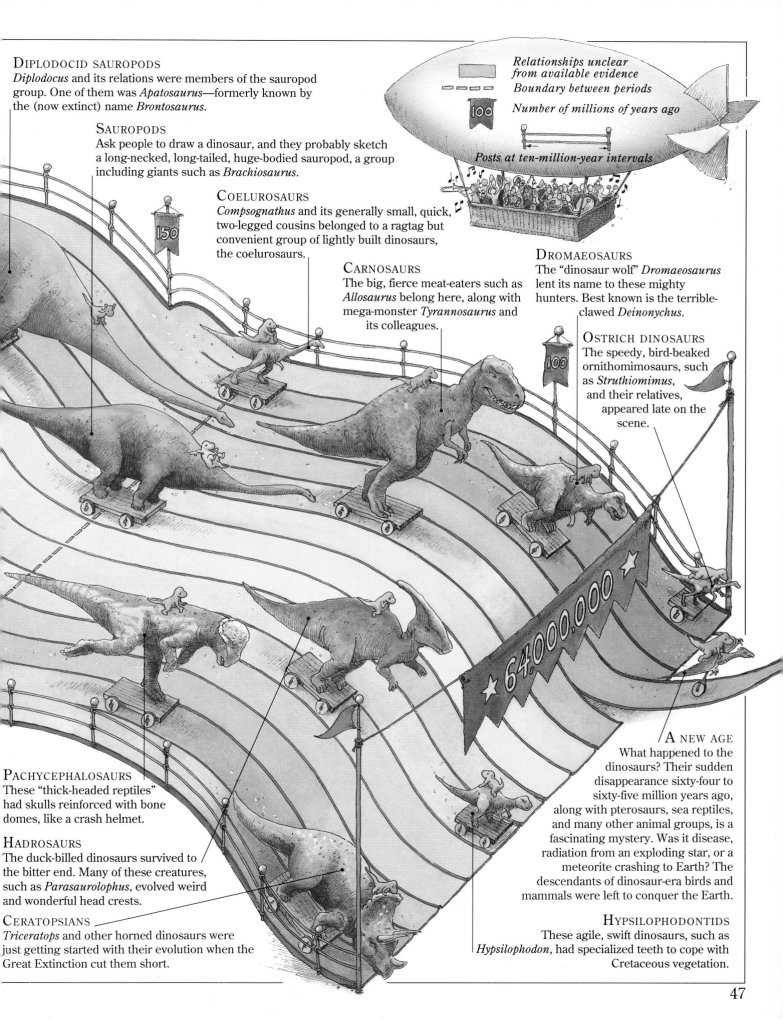

DIPLODOCID SAUROPODS
Diplodocus and its relations were members of the sauropod group. One of them was *Apatosaurus*—formerly known by the (now extinct) name *Brontosaurus*.

SAUROPODS
Ask people to draw a dinosaur, and they probably sketch a long-necked, long-tailed, huge-bodied sauropod, a group including giants such as *Brachiosaurus*.

COELUROSAURS
Compsognathus and its generally small, quick, two-legged cousins belonged to a ragtag but convenient group of lightly built dinosaurs, the coelurosaurs.

CARNOSAURS
The big, fierce meat-eaters such as *Allosaurus* belong here, along with mega-monster *Tyrannosaurus* and its colleagues.

Relationships unclear from available evidence
Boundary between periods
Number of millions of years ago

Posts at ten-million-year intervals

DROMAEOSAURS
The "dinosaur wolf" *Dromaeosaurus* lent its name to these mighty hunters. Best known is the terrible-clawed *Deinonychus*.

OSTRICH DINOSAURS
The speedy, bird-beaked ornithomimosaurs, such as *Struthiomimus*, and their relatives, appeared late on the scene.

64,000,000

PACHYCEPHALOSAURS
These "thick-headed reptiles" had skulls reinforced with bone domes, like a crash helmet.

HADROSAURS
The duck-billed dinosaurs survived to the bitter end. Many of these creatures, such as *Parasaurolophus*, evolved weird and wonderful head crests.

CERATOPSIANS
Triceratops and other horned dinosaurs were just getting started with their evolution when the Great Extinction cut them short.

A NEW AGE
What happened to the dinosaurs? Their sudden disappearance sixty-four to sixty-five million years ago, along with pterosaurs, sea reptiles, and many other animal groups, is a fascinating mystery. Was it disease, radiation from an exploding star, or a meteorite crashing to Earth? The descendants of dinosaur-era birds and mammals were left to conquer the Earth.

HYPSILOPHODONTIDS
These agile, swift dinosaurs, such as *Hypsilophodon*, had specialized teeth to cope with Cretaceous vegetation.

INDEX

ACKNOWLEDGMENTS

The illustrator and author would like to thank:
• The staff at the Zoological Society's Wolfson Library and the Natural History Museum, London, for their help and courtesy
• Sue Tunnicliff for her animal training

• Helen Cooper, who posed for the mini-dinos

Dorling Kindersley would like to thank: Miranda Smith for editorial help, Jane Parker for the index, and Neil Palfreyman for production guidance